MY PIZZA

MY PIZZA

the easy no-knead way to make spectacular pizza at home

Jim Lahey

founder of Sullivan Street Bakery and Co.

WITH RICK FLASTE

clarkson potter/publishers

NEW YORK

Dedicated in loving memory
to my dad,
DICK LAHEY

Copyright © 2012 by Jim Lahey
Photographs copyright © 2012 by Squire Fox

Published in the United States by Clarkson Potter/
Publishers, an imprint of the Crown Publishing Group,
a division of Random House, Inc., New York.
www.crownpublishing.com
www.clarksonpotter.com

CLARKSON POTTER is a trademark and POTTER with
colophon is a registered trademark of Random House,
Inc.

Library of Congress Cataloging-in-Publication Data
Lahey, Jim.
  My pizza / Jim Lahey with Rick Flaste. — 1st ed.
  Includes index.
  1. Pizza.   I. Flaste, Rick.   II. Title.
  TX770.P58L34   2012
  641.8'248—dc23   2011019842

ISBN 978-0-307-88615-6
eISBN 978-0-307-95323-0

Printed in China

Book and jacket design by Stephanie Huntwork
Interior and jacket photography by Squire Fox

10 9 8 7 6 5 4 3 2 1

First Edition

CONTENTS

INTRODUCTION

In the early days of my Manhattan pizza restaurant, a middle-aged woman came through the front door, her eyes widened by the crowd that had been drawn to the place even before it had officially opened. She was wearing a huge white hairy coat—which meant she was going to take up about two spots at one of the long communal tables. She wedged herself in and ordered a pie—I think it was a Margherita—and as soon as it arrived she called over the manager. She told him that nothing about the pizza was the way it was "supposed" to be. It had too little sauce, she said. The crust was too dark, and it was too firm besides.

As anyone who has baked from my book *My Bread*—based on my method for a stunningly easy, rustic no-knead loaf—already knows, I usually diverge from the well-worn road and travel my own way.

That's not to say that, in creating my pizzas, I'm coming to them without an authentic background. I've spent many months traveling throughout Italy, always learning as I go, searching for the bread and pizza standards that appeal most to my own sensibility, my palate, and my strong (some would say headstrong) feelings about the art of cooking and baking. My first trip to Rome just blew me away—the beauty, the produce, the bread. Of course, I've also been to Naples (the Italian pizza's heartland), but I definitely don't want you to think this book is some kind of grab-bag of Neapolitan pizzas. As much as I admire the intense appreciation for ingredients there, I have frequently been disappointed by the pizzas, many of which appeal to a tourist-grade lowest common denominator. In a nation of such beauty and—in the good times—affluence, Naples has stood out too regularly for its episodes of crime and poverty. Too many pizza bakers don't worry much about whether the tomatoes in the sauce are the best, as long as they are cheap; the mozzarella they choose is too often of poor quality, lacking in moisture. They don't bother to give the dough time enough to ferment properly, settling for a mediocre crust.

Pizza deserves respect and admiration—for everything about it, but especially the bread, the crust. As a former art student who turned to baking, I see a pizza crust as a canvas, an invitation to paint and sculpt with food. I hope that doesn't sound too pretentious; pizza is after all a peasant food, but a glorious peasant food when someone approaches it with care and affection, taking bread and building it into a beautiful whole meal.

As much carping as I've just done about Naples, I have to say it is pizza paradise compared to the United States. If you choose carefully, you *can* find great pizza in Naples. Back home, however, I want to weep when I think how industrialized

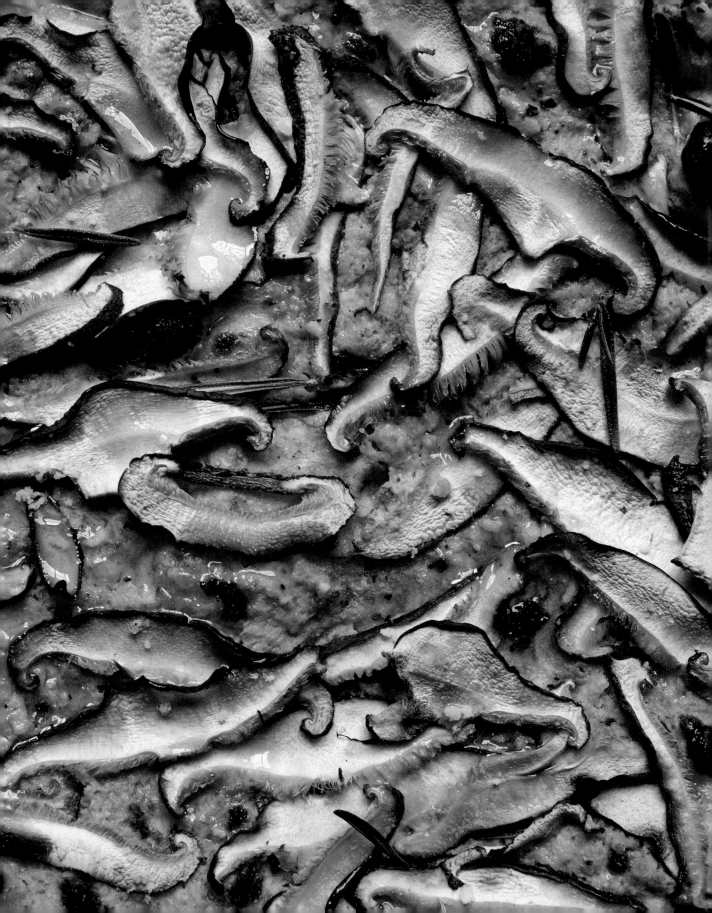

(with a few exceptions) this simple food has become. Many Americans grow up with the notion that real pizza is the stuff they box at Pizza Hut or Domino's—pizza for which the greatest objective seems to be how fast a truck can get it to one's door. Or it's a notion formed by the so-called pizza parlor. Isn't a "parlor" supposed to suggest a pleasant place where bright people gather to talk, enjoy each other's company, share ideas? A beauty parlor offers more creativity than your average American pizza parlor, a garish, harried place where floppy pies made from trashy ingredients are turned out over and over again—until customers are persuaded that this experience is somehow a good thing.

I've been fortunate enough to find and learn from the genuine article in many places. In Naples, when you manage to squeeze past all the bad stuff, there is Da Michele, a nondescript yet renowned and worshipped place that seems to reserve all its skill for selecting the purest, freshest ingredients and then assembling them basically, without pretension. I also learned from Chris Bianco, the award-winning chef at Pizzeria Bianco in Phoenix, who puts most boastful New Yorkers to shame, and from the inventive Andrew Feinberg at Franny's in Brooklyn. They are all wonderfully expert in their personal ways, and the education they shared with me helped put me on the path to making pizza my way.

I came to pizza baking slowly. First, I was a bread baker. And in some ways bread saved my life. It fulfilled so many needs, gave me purpose, allowed me to indulge a talent that I must have had in me all along. I opened Sullivan Street Bakery in New York City's SoHo neighborhood in 1994; in the fall of 2000, we moved the bakery to a larger location in Hell's Kitchen. As I struggled through my early mornings, year after year, I was always learning and inventing. Along the way, I developed my no-knead home-kitchen process for dough that, once risen, is cooked in a preheated pot in the oven; the pot acts as an oven within an oven, creating a dark, rustic crust while at the same time keeping the crumb moist. A little yeast and extended fermentation strengthen the dough, eliminating the kneading step that's supposed to do the same thing. It's a method that ultimately brought me widespread recognition—in large part thanks to Mark Bittman's article about it in the *New York Times,* a piece that, on the wings of the Internet, flew around the world so fast and so far that even Mark was startled. That was in 2006.

But, earlier, soon after September 11, I got the idea that I'd like to do something to cheer people up. On New Year's Day, while gloom still gripped the city, I decided to act on it: I threw a pizza party at the bakery. I made pizzas that were round, charred at the edge, and relatively firm on the bottom (I don't like soft crusts with the toppings sliding off). It was too soon to think about using my no-knead dough, an approach that hadn't advanced far enough yet. That would come later (and is now in fact the foundation of my crusts). I invited friends, chefs, and customers. And the party caught on. I threw that party every New Year's for four years.

I was a baker, not a chef, and yet . . . I got it in my head that I wanted to be able to show off a bit more of my cooking skills beyond bread making—as much as I do revere it. So I persuaded a friend who had a pizza truck to go with me to Union Square, the great farmer's market in the city. The pizzas I made there—and gave away free, which admittedly is always a surefire approach—were simple: the Rosa, a Margherita, and the spinach pizza I call a Popeye, all of which you'll see in this book. The hungry natives lined up five deep. I also gave away T-shirts that shouted "Viva Hell's Kitchen" to announce the bakery's new address.

As for the pizza, I knew at that moment, as I feverishly turned out one pizza after another, that I could really pull this thing off for a whole lot of people. And the idea of a restaurant—an exceptional, inventive restaurant that would break the mold of the commonplace New York pizzeria—was more powerful than ever in my mind. I remember the date clearly. It was November 1, a soft Indian summer day; seven days later Mark's piece on my no-knead bread ran in the *Times*. The glow of that article was definitely helpful when it came time to create a restaurant. Everything was coming together.

As I approached my new Manhattan pizza place, Co. (for company), which would open in early 2009, I became obsessed with pizza. I kept thinking about the whole spectrum of Italian combinations of sauces, meats, and cheeses, many of them most familiar as dressings for pasta, and transformed them into novel pizza pies.

In the past, for the most part, the few pizzas I made to sell at my bakery next to the loaves were rectangular pizzas in the Roman style. They especially worked well for a retail store, where they might have to sit around awhile. A beautiful aspect of these relatively thick pies is that they are durable—snacks designed to be eaten hot or at room temperature or even the next day. But with the restaurant, I was drawn to the best of the thinner, crisper, disk-shaped pies of Naples, the ones that are so seductive hot and fresh from the oven. There is a touch of the spiritual in that disk; it's an unforced, natural shape that reminds me of a pool of rainwater, of da Vinci's man of perfect proportions, or of the mandala, a symbol of harmony and spirituality. And these round pies are elegant besides—the toppings carefully placed, with a charred, blistered rim forming a dramatic, stark frame for the ingredients.

I should pause for a second and say that although I've been describing the pies as round here, I don't mean a perfect circle. Each pizza is handmade and, as such, idiosyncratic. From a purely functional point of view, they are shaped to be easy to cut into wedges. But I suppose it would be more accurate to call them "roundish." When I see a cook laboring to perfect that shape, I see an individual who is perhaps too involved with the circle at the expense of the ingredients.

With this book, I expect you to be able to make pizzas at home every bit as attractive and alive with flavor as the ones I produce in the restaurant and my own home kitchen. The pies should look terrific and they should be fun —like the Bird's Nest Pie, which boasts shaved asparagus with cheese and quail eggs, or the Pepperoni Pie, which has no pepperoni sausage on it, but rather a red pepper puree with a topping of lamb sausage meat. I want you to see how unfussy just a handful of familiar ingredients can be, and yet how transcendent, if selected and combined with skill. (That's the true miracle of genuine Italian cooking—elevating the ordinary to the extraordinary.) And, of course, while I'll teach you how to use a very basic tomato sauce, I'll also demonstrate how to free yourself from that base with pizzas you may never have imagined before.

I hope you will engage in this adventure with high spirit, optimism, and anticipation. Don't be intimidated; making a pizza is not haute cuisine. It requires surprisingly little effort—remember, we'll be relying on my simple no-knead bread recipe for the crust—and, once the toppings have been prepared, just a few minutes of cooking. After you've mastered my home kitchen techniques (I broil rather than bake, for instance) and experienced the excitement of a deeply flavored, often innovative pizza, let your own creativity take flight. I hope you'll come up with pizzas—beautiful, simple constructions—you can call your own. I'll know I've done my job when you come to see pizza as healthy, artful, and so infinitely variable that you wouldn't mind eating a pizza pie just about every day, like I do!

To amplify that sense of variety, I've complemented the pizzas in this book with a selection of bright, often unusual salads, toasts, soups, and desserts—most of them directly off the menu at Co.—that can round out or extend a meal. They're going to be especially welcome when you're entertaining.

I feel so intensely about what I'm trying to do that I implore you to be in touch with me directly, at my website, theuniversityofbread.com. Let me know how it's going. If anything is confusing, tell me, and I'll do my best to clear it up. If you want to try something of your own invention but are unsure about the combination you have in mind, I'll give you an honest opinion. I'm really looking forward to this, our time together.

EQUIPMENT

I have the feeling that many home cooks think that making great, restaurant-quality pizza in a conventional kitchen is either impossible or involves too much special equipment. Not true. The few pieces of important equipment are easily available and relatively inexpensive. There is a bit of cleverness involved however: Just look at how I boost the surface temperature of my pizza stone during the preheating stage by baking it and then broiling it.

THE BEAUTY OF STONE

First you'll need a pizza stone; these are inexpensive and readily available online and in kitchenware stores. I prefer a commercial one that is ¾ inch thick because it holds the heat better than thinner ones. But the most commonly available stones are ½ inch thick; I've developed these recipes on them and find they function well. These pizza stones are usually 14 × 16-inch rectangles, and this is excellent for a single pizza. They also have the advantage of being easier to handle than anything larger would be—and they fit into any oven. (You can even create your own pizza stone using kiln tile.) My heating method is to preheat the stone, first on bake at 500°F, and then under the broiler, so the surface has climbed to well over 600°F by the time you call on it to do its work.

THAT INDISPENSABLE PEEL

In addition to the stone, you'll find it's extremely useful to have a pizza peel (or paddle). It's an inexpensive, easy-to-find tool that helps enormously for getting the pies on and off the stone. In the recipes, I always tell you to flour the peel well so that the raw dough will slide easily (thanks to quick, jerking motions as you transfer it) from peel to stone. Peels come in a number of materials. Most of the time, I stick to the wooden model designed for the home, with a short handle that's only 8 or 10 inches long—not the huge tool the professionals use, and probably the one you have in mind. I also like to keep a large metal spatula nearby. It's helpful for rotating the pie if it's cooking unevenly or for transferring it from the stone to the peel if you're finding that awkward, though usually a quick thrust of the peel will do the trick. It's also handy for scraping any burnt crust off a well-used stone (the stone should be kept as clean as possible but not washed).

THE BLADES FOR THE JOB

For slicing the pie into wedges, a pizza wheel is excellent. So is a large mezzaluna (the half-moon-shaped blade with a handle at either end); a sharp chef's knife works just fine, too.

In preparing the pizza toppings, there are times when you'll need to slice ingredients very thinly. A mandoline—the slide-shaped

tool with a blade embedded in it—is best for this. The classic and expensive French version has pretty much given way throughout the world of cooking to the inexpensive Japanese models, which do a wonderful job. But you'll get by most of the time with a sharp knife or your food processor. Alternatively, turn to the underused slicing blade on the old-fashioned box grater, my favorite tool of all. There's something wonderful about having an implement as basic and versatile as this in your hands. Generations have relied on it without complaint (except about the occasional skinned knuckle).

MEASURING—THE VIRTUES OF A SCALE

Many of you already have a home kitchen scale, but many of you don't. If you're in the second group, I urge you to get one. They generally cost less than a decent pan and are available in every kitchenware shop—online, too, of course. I'm a big believer in weighing ingredients, using the metric system in almost every case, even for liquids—rather than the familiar ounces, tablespoons, cups, and other measurements known as the U.S. Customary System. Weighing is more accurate and—once you get the knack of doing it regularly—faster. But in case I haven't persuaded you, you'll find both sets of measurements for ingredients in this book. Although they often don't *exactly* equal each other (it's the nature of the systems), they're always very close.

A REVERENCE FOR INGREDIENTS

The best pizzas are made from simple yet impeccable ingredients, carefully put together. The dough is paramount, of course, but so are the toppings, in particular the cheeses, tomatoes, and olive oil.

FLOUR WITHOUT FUSS

You may be wondering how picky you have to be in buying flour for the crust. All sorts of "pizza flours" inhabit the shelves of stores near you, and there is a lot of carrying on about the flour when people strike poses in a discourse about pizza. But you don't need all these highly specialized flours. I get perfectly fine results using common bread flour or all-purpose flour and have no emphatic preference. In the recipes in this book, for simplicity's sake, I specify all-purpose.

OLIVE OIL *WITH* FUSS

As for olive oil, so prevalent in pizza making, I do want to carry on a bit. The first thing I'm concerned about is, of course, flavor. Olive oil is like wine or great bread—more complex than you might imagine, more layered. The best and freshest extra-virgin oil (that is, from the first pressing of the olives and not from what's left behind after that step) should be smooth and a touch buttery. As you taste it by itself, the middle of the experience will be clean on the palate and fruity, and just at the end, the "finish," there should be a sense of pepper, a bit of spice. The good oils are produced in many countries; Italy,

Spain, and France come to mind first. But Australian oil can be fine and so can that of South Africa. My absolute favorite, however, is Chilean. Italy may have the richest olive oil culture; Chile has the highest standards.

Buying really good olive oil is a much trickier business than it seems. Sure, the label may say "E.V.O." and it may say "Italian," but you need to read the fine print. A lot of Italian olive oil is actually just blended and packaged in Italy. It could come from anywhere. Often it contains oil that is old and cheap. Look to see if the label goes beyond the "imported from Italy" designation to be much more specific about the country, region, or farm where it was produced. It should be exclusively from a single reputable place. That's a good indication of care and quality.

THOSE ESSENTIAL CHEESES

The cheeses named throughout should always be of the highest quality. The role they play is so central to a great pizza you can't afford to skimp. If it's mozzarella, whether imported or domestic, make sure it's fresh, and more—it should be creamy, slightly sour, and very wet, with a fleshy texture.

I always call for Parmigiano-Reggiano as the Parmesan cheese; you can also use Grana Padano, pretty much its equal. The other stuff that passes for Parmesan in supermarkets—no matter how convenient the packaging—is unspeakably inferior.

The pecorino fresco I call for in some recipes is the youngest of this sheep's-milk cheese, often aged for less than a month; it's softer and less salty than the cheeses aged significantly longer. It's available in many good cheese or Italian specialty stores (pecorino fresco is a staple in Tuscany) and, if those sources fail you, it can be readily ordered online. Also, don't worry if the pecorino is anywhere from one month to six months old. That's still young in my book and will be pleasing on a pie.

TOMATO PERFECTION

Excellent tomatoes are—no surprise—the key to great tomato sauces. The citizens of Naples, when they do good work and resist the urge to stint, are glowingly proud of their tomatoes—San Marzano tomatoes, for the most part, grown on the plains south of Mount Vesuvius. Of course, I believe in using the best fresh tomatoes available, too. Depending on the season and where you live, they can come from Florida or the Hudson Valley or your own backyard. But if you're tempted to settle for distinctly inferior out-of-season fresh tomatoes, go for the canned instead, preferably from Italy.

With fresh tomatoes, one word to pay special attention to in the ingredient list for red sauce is *ripe*. By that I mean, among other qualities, completely red. A ripe tomato will peel much more easily than an underipe one. Also, be sure it has the sweet, slightly acidic flavor common to all great tomatoes. (I'm well aware that some tomatoes are designed not to be acidic, but that's not what we're talking about here.)

ANCHOVIES, PACKED WELL

I am a fan of anchovies and they frequently show up in my recipes for pizzas and salads (although if you hate them you can, in some instances, leave them out). I always stipulate salt-packed anchovies, which are not what you see most often in the supermarket (those are packed in salted, sometimes rancid oil). The simply salt-packed ones are more flavorful and firmer, and they allow you to rely exclusively on your own very good extra-virgin olive oil when required by a recipe. They do involve a bit of extra work. You'll need to rinse off the salt, dry, and fillet them with a paring knife, removing the spine and innards. To find salt-packed anchovies you'll have to pay a visit to a specialty store or order them online. If all you've got on hand is the oil-packed ones, however, go ahead. They'll work, but you'll lose a certain subtlety.

ADJUSTING FOR OVEN TYPE

The recipes—including preheating and cooking times—were developed using a high-quality home gas oven with a broiler at the top of the primary compartment. But even if that's the sort of oven you own, too, it could well vary from mine in the heat it produces during preheating and baking. As a practical matter, what this means is that cooking times are simply guidelines; some pies will take longer in your oven than specified and some less.

For a properly cooked pizza, keep the visual cues in mind and check: The pizza is finished when the surface is bubbling and the rim is deeply charred but not actually burnt. (Don't worry about losing heat if you open the oven to peek in.) Try a simple pie first—one with few toppings—so you learn just how your own oven works before moving on to the more elaborate creations. And keep in mind that the last thing you want is toppings that are uncooked.

Whatever oven you're using, the applicable technique should become second nature after one or two tries.

ELECTRIC VARIATION

Many of you will be working with an electric oven, a slightly different experience from gas. The elements of the electric ones are generally designed to turn off when the oven reaches 500°F or 550°F and the door is closed—even if it's the broiler doing the heating and not the baking element. When you completely understand how I use my gas broiler continuously to force the stone hotter on the surface and also to cook the pizza (door closed) so the crust chars properly and the toppings cook quickly, the electric's shutdown feature may strike you as a potential problem. It's easily solved. Thanks mostly to the tireless efforts of Amanda, our recipe tester (who also, while cooking every pizza in the book, devised some of the serving strategies that follow), we figured out how to overcome this bump in the road. It's a relatively simple matter that requires some adjustments in the timing and procedure.

With electric ovens that turn off at 500°F or so, place the stone on a rack about 4 inches from the top heating element (not the 8 inches called for with gas) and preheat, on bake, at 500°F for the usual 30 minutes. Then, to boost the heat of the stone without the oven's elements shutting down, open the oven door a few inches and leave it ajar for about 30 seconds. Some of the ambient heat will escape, but the stone will stay just as hot. Now close the oven door and switch to broil for 10 minutes to heat the surface to the maximum. Open the door and slide the pizza in to

broil. Because the stone is so close to the element, you may need to pull the rack out a few inches to get the pie centered on the stone; do it quickly and don't worry about losing too much heat. With the door closed, broil for roughly 2 minutes longer than specified for gas—until the crust is adequately charred but not burnt and the toppings are bubbling. Remember, it's the visual cues that count most. Check a couple of times; the pizza will cook quickly. The broiler, in our testing, did in fact remain on for the entire cooking period using this method, and the pies turned out perfectly.

BOTTOM BROILER

For those of you—many fewer these days than used to be the case—with a gas broiler in a bottom drawer of the oven, here's what to do: Start with the stone in the broiler at the lowest level or on the floor of the oven. Preheat on low for about 20 minutes, and then switch to high for another 5 minutes. Slide in the pizza, close the drawer, and broil as instructed by the recipe (most often 3½ to 4 minutes), until bubbling and properly charred—checking to be sure it's not burning.

SERVING STRATEGIES

If you have your dough ready and want to make a pie quickly, turn to the No Sauce Pizzas chapter (page 93) for the quickest recipes. For many of these pies, particularly those with red or white sauce, you'll probably be happier if you make your tomato sauce or béchamel ahead. All the basic ingredient recipes are in the Toppings chapter (page 115) or close to where they're called for. With the supporting cast already in the wings, the pizzas take just a few minutes to throw together and cook at showtime.

Each pizza, cut into four wedges, is meant to be one substantial portion. Since one stone will accommodate only a single pie—and it's very likely you'll be serving more than yourself—we've devised a number of strategies that work well for a group. The key is that the pies take only a few minutes each to cook.

For dinner for, say, four people, cook a single pizza, slice it, serve everybody a wedge, and then sit for a while to enjoy it yourself before returning to the kitchen to prepare another. To make the process more efficient, have several balls of floured dough waiting near your work area, covered with a damp cloth to prevent drying. Shape each one as needed, slip it onto a peel, top it, and cook. If you're hosting a dinner party, set out some of the toasts or salads on the table so there's always something to nibble on during the meal while the pizzas keep coming, a few minutes apart.

The most fun of all when you're serving a group is to have a kitchen party, if your kitchen is large enough to allow people to stand around comfortably or perch on stools at an island. Cook each pizza—to the inevitable oohs and ahs of guests who can't believe such fantastic-looking pizzas are coming out of your regular oven—and serve them right there. Let guests take turns assembling and cooking the pies. Actually, you should expect some to plead for a try. The pizza making becomes the party's entertainment.

If your oven is on the larger side and can accommodate two stones at once, side by side on the rack, you can prepare two pies at the same time. With two stones at work, you may decide to serve just half a pie to each of four diners, along with salads and toasts. It will be plenty. Depending on how practiced you become, it's possible to serve eight or even ten guests in a single evening, but more than that and you'll end up feeling like the frantic guy at the local pizzeria, which would defeat the purpose.

The temptation, of course, is to make several pies and hold off serving them until all are cooked; there's no crime in that—many of them will survive just fine—but I've been assuming you want to serve each pie fresh and hot.

BEER AND WINE: A RELAXED POINT OF VIEW Although I have my personal favorites, I'm usually reluctant to urge a pairing of a particular wine or beer with a pizza. But I do like to think in terms of just a few guiding principles.

The reason almost any good beer will go well has to do with its most fundamental characteristics. The carbonation scrubs the palate and the beer's malt is a delicate echo of the malt emanating from the charred crust of the pie. But some assertive pizzas—like my Brussels Sprouts and Chestnut Pie (page 89)—will especially benefit from a big, spicy beer. The Belgian style generally works well here. The sweeter, more delicate pies—such as Onion Pie (page 84)—are enhanced by a beer that can't overwhelm them. A light lager or a mild ale usually comes to mind.

As for wine, it's pretty difficult to go wrong with anything that's decent. The whites, naturally, tend to go best with the milder pizzas, the reds with the heartier ones. But, in the end, my advice—with beer or wine—is to go with what you like.

PIZZA PIES

In the humdrum world of the formulaic pizza, tomato sauce seems to be nearly universal. Of course, tomato sauce is a good thing—no debating that. But it's not the *only* thing. If it were, it would limit what we could create—and for many pizza makers it does. Think about how unimaginative pasta would be if absolutely every dish had to start with tomato sauce instead of the alternative possibilities presented by olive oil, wine, or cream. So I classify my pizzas as based on red sauce (almost always a very basic tomato preparation), white sauce (the flour-milk-butter mixture known as a béchamel), or no sauce at all. If you start thinking with these options in mind, it sets free the creative cook inside your mind, and the possibilities are endless.

THE PIZZA DOUGH FOUNDATION

I know how great the lure of dough from the grocery store must be, and I won't hate you if you turn to it out of lack of time or planning. (A pound of frozen dough should be enough for two pizzas.) But it will not give you the kind of crisp, beautiful, flavorful crust mine will; the moisture content will be different, the cooking time may be different, and so will the texture. (Also, beware of additives lurking in the stuff.) It will be decidedly inferior. And why turn to the premade when mine is so easy to make? Yes, my recipe does have to be started a day ahead, but then it just sits, on its own, until the next day when it is prepared and waiting for your creation.

pizza dough

MAKES 4 BALLS OF
MAKES 4 BALLS OF DOUGH, ENOUGH FOR 4 PIZZAS • While I'm not picky about the flour—either bread flour or all-purpose is fine—what does concern me is how the dough is handled. Treat it gently so the dough holds its character, its texture. When you get around to shaping the disk for a pie, go easy as you stretch it to allow it to retain a bit of bumpiness (I think of it as blistering), so not all of the gas is smashed out of the fermented dough. I prefer to hold off on shaping the ball until just before topping it. If it's going to sit for a while—more than a couple of minutes—cover it with a damp kitchen towel to prevent it from drying out.

I offer you two approaches for shaping. The simpler one, executed completely on the work surface, is slower than the second, where you lift the disk in the air and stretch it by rotating it on your knuckles. Lifting it into the air to shape it is more fun, too.

500 grams (17½ ounces or about 3¾ cups) **all-purpose flour**, plus more for shaping the dough

1 gram (¼ teaspoon) **active dry yeast**

16 grams (2 teaspoons) **fine sea salt**

350 grams (1½ cups) **water**

1 In a medium bowl, thoroughly blend the flour, yeast, and salt. Add the water and, with a wooden spoon or your hands, mix thoroughly.

2 Cover the bowl with plastic wrap or a kitchen towel and allow it to rise at room temperature (about 72°F) for 18 hours or until it has more than doubled. It will take longer in a chilly room and less time in a very warm one.

3 Flour a work surface and scrape out the dough. Divide it into 4 equal parts and shape them: For each portion, start with the right side of the dough and pull it toward the center; then do the same with the left, then the top, then the bottom. (The order doesn't actually matter; what you want is four folds.) Shape each portion into a round and turn seam side down. Mold the dough into a neat circular mound. The mounds should not be sticky; if they are, dust with more flour.

4 If you don't intend to use the dough right away, wrap the balls individually in plastic and refrigerate for up to 3 days. Return to room temperature by leaving them out on the counter, covered in a damp cloth, for 2 to 3 hours before needed.

NOTE Don't freeze the dough, but you can store it in the refrigerator, wrapped in plastic, for up to three days. In effect, when you're set to use it, you have your own ready-made dough.

SHAPING THE DISK (METHOD 1)

Take one ball of the dough and generously flour it, your hands, and the work surface. Then press it down and gently stretch it out to 6 to 8 inches. Very carefully continue the process, massaging it into a roundish disk of 10 to 12 inches, stroking and shaping with the palms of your hands and with your fingers. Don't handle it more than necessary, though; you want some of the gas bubbles to remain in the dough. It should look slightly blistered. Flour the peel and lift the disk onto the center. The dough is now ready to be topped.

SHAPING THE DISK (METHOD 2)

Take one ball of the dough and generously flour it, your hands, and the work surface. Then press it down and gently stretch it out to 6 to 8 inches. Supporting the disk with your knuckles toward the outer edge and lifting it above the work surface, keep stretching the dough by rotating it with your knuckles, gently pulling it wider and wider until the disk reaches 10 to 12 inches. (See photos, page 28.) Set the disk on a well-floured peel. It is now ready to be topped.

whole wheat pizza dough

Any of pizzas in this book can be made with whole wheat dough, although I've found over the years that I personally prefer less whole wheat in the mixture than others might. Too much of it, to my taste, makes the crust gritty.

To make whole wheat dough, use two-thirds white flour to one-third whole wheat, and double the yeast used in the standard pizza dough recipe.

Pepperoni Pie

RED SAUCE PIZZAS

basic tomato sauce 34

tomato pie 37

rosa pie 38

margherita pie 41

stracciatella pie 42

amalfi pie 45

spicy eggplant pie 46

fennel and sausage pie 49

giardiniera pie 50

radicchio pie 52

zucchini pie 53

veal meatball pie 55

amatriciana pie 57

boscaiola pie 58

pepperoni pie 61

This collection of red sauce—based pizzas is diverse and, I'm sure, so inventive you never imagined some of these combinations before. That said, it would be ridiculous to neglect the beloved classics like the Margherita or the Rosa—I just try to give them my personal touch. In the ingredients section (page 17), I make the point that you need to search for tomato excellence—ripe and acidic/sweet—wherever you find it, whether in Italy or your own backyard. And if you can't find that kind of perfection, go with the best canned tomatoes you can buy (or turn to the two other pizza chapters in this book). My basic sauce is so very simple and pure that an inferior tomato will be beyond useless.

basic tomato sauce

MAKES 620 TO 800
GRAMS (DEPENDING ON
WHETHER YOU USE FRESH
OR CANNED TOMATOES,
WHICH YIELD A GREATER
VOLUME); OR ENOUGH
FOR ABOUT 8 PIZZAS •

This tomato sauce is really
not much more than pulped
tomatoes. Nevertheless, in
all its simplicity, it is an ideal
foundation for many pizzas
because the toppings that
will go over it and blend with
it bring a bouquet of flavors
to the pie. I don't want the
sauce and toppings fighting
each other. Harmony: That's
my mantra.

700 grams (1½ pounds) **ripe plum tomatoes** or
1 794-gram (28-ounce) can **peeled Italian plum tomatoes**

20 grams (about 2 tablespoons) **extra-virgin olive oil**

2 grams (¼ teaspoon) **fine sea salt**

1 If using fresh tomatoes, bring 4 quarts water to a boil in a 5- to 6-quart pot.

2 Cut away the dry stem area of the tomatoes, leaving the core intact. Place 2 or 3 tomatoes at a time in the boiling water for 5 to 10 seconds. Remove with a slotted spoon and put on a rack to cool. Peel the tomatoes with a paring knife.

3 Whether using fresh or canned, cut each tomato into several wedges and run them through a food mill over a medium bowl to create a pulp (not a fine puree; you want to retain some texture). If you don't have a food mill, just squish them with your hands—it's messy but fun.

4 Stir in the olive oil and salt. The sauce will keep, covered, in the refrigerator for up to 1 week.

1 ball of **Pizza Dough**, shaped and waiting on a floured peel (page 26)

70 grams (¼ cup) **Basic Tomato Sauce** (page 34)

Generous pinch of **fine sea salt**

Extra-virgin olive oil, for drizzling

1 Put the pizza stone on a rack in a gas oven about 8 inches from the broiler. Preheat the oven on bake at 500°F for 30 minutes. Switch to broil for 10 minutes. (For an electric variation, see page 18.)

2 With the dough on the peel, spoon the tomato sauce over the surface and spread it evenly, leaving about an inch of the rim untouched. Sprinkle with salt. Drizzle oil over the pie.

3 With quick, jerking motions, slide the pie onto the stone. Broil for 3 minutes under gas (somewhat longer with an electric oven; see page 18), until the top is bubbling and the crust is nicely charred but not burnt.

4 Using the peel, transfer the pizza to a tray or serving platter before slicing it into wedges. Serve immediately.

MAKES ONE 10- TO 12-INCH PIZZA • It may be a good idea to make this elemental tomato pizza first (it's a tossup between this and the Starter White Pie on page 67), before moving on to anything else. I know that at first blush it seems too simple to be good, mostly just sauce and bread. But even if you doubt me now, I don't think you will later. This pie is great practice for preparing the dough and learning my cooking method. And as you try one pie after another, you'll also begin to get the idea of how I construct a pizza. If I start by thinking about this unadorned tomato version, for instance, I know that with a simple addition of flavorings it can easily be transformed into the Rosa (page 38). Or, I might use cheese and arugula (the Stracciatella, page 42) or olives and anchovy (the Amalfi, page 45). It's all a matter of imagination, something like architecture; you build a base and go from there.

rosa pie

MAKES ONE 10- TO 12-INCH PIZZA • With my Rosa pizza, I boost that basic Tomato Pie on page 37 with garlic and chili along with some fresh oregano (if it's available). And, with just those small additional touches, something quite distinct is created. You get more bite, more complexity. The Rosa is terrific for entertaining because it's surprisingly satisfying and extremely easy—allowing you to expend most of your energy on a subsequent pie or two requiring greater concentration.

1 ball of **Pizza Dough**, shaped and waiting on a floured peel (page 26)

70 grams (¼ cup) **Basic Tomato Sauce** (page 34)

Generous pinch of **fine sea salt**

Pinch of **chili flakes**

1 medium **garlic clove**, thinly slivered

Extra-virgin olive oil, for drizzling

4 or 5 fresh **oregano leaves**, chopped (optional)

1 Put the pizza stone on a rack in a gas oven about 8 inches from the broiler. Preheat the oven on bake at 500°F for 30 minutes. Switch to broil for 10 minutes. (For an electric variation, see page 18.)

2 With the dough on the peel, spoon the tomato sauce over the surface and spread it evenly, leaving about an inch of the rim untouched. Sprinkle with salt and chili flakes. Distribute the garlic evenly over the pie. Drizzle with oil.

3 With quick, jerking motions, slide the pie onto the stone. Broil for 3 minutes under gas (somewhat longer with an electric oven; see page 18), until the top is bubbling and the crust is nicely charred but not burnt.

4 Using the peel, transfer the pizza to a tray or serving platter. Sprinkle with the oregano, if using. Slice and serve immediately.

margherita pie

1 ball of **Pizza Dough**, shaped and waiting on a floured peel (page 26)

70 grams (¼ cup) **Basic Tomato Sauce** (page 34)

200 grams (7 ounces) fresh **mozzarella**, pulled into 10 to 12 clumps

10 grams (3 tablespoons) finely grated **Parmigiano-Reggiano cheese**

Pinch of **fine sea salt**

6 **basil leaves**, or to taste

MAKES ONE 10- TO 12-INCH PIZZA • This is among the most familiar of Neapolitan pizzas, often just tomato sauce and cheese baked on a disk of flatbread. In cities like New York, the Margherita has been trashed by the ubiquitous ordinary pizza parlor—often through a lack of attention in cooking and a careless approach to ingredients. But if you're lucky enough to discover one of the really good pizza places in Naples or elsewhere in Italy, you'll see an almost fanatical approach to the pizza's components. The tomatoes will likely be San Marzanos; the mozzarella will be from the best buffalo milk. I too am determined to use the highest-quality ingredients I can get. But, when it comes to mozzarella, I've learned cow's milk can also produce some great cheese. And you probably remember how fanatical I am about excellence in tomatoes!

1 Put the pizza stone on a rack in a gas oven about 8 inches from the broiler. Preheat the oven on bake at 500°F for 30 minutes. Switch to broil for 10 minutes. (For an electric variation, see page 18.)

2 With the dough on the peel, spoon the tomato sauce over the surface and spread it evenly, leaving about an inch of the rim untouched. Distribute the mozzarella evenly over the pie.

3 With quick, jerking motions, slide the pie onto the stone. Broil for 3½ to 4 minutes under gas (somewhat longer with an electric oven; see page 18), until the top is bubbling and the crust is nicely charred but not burnt.

4 Using the peel, transfer the pizza to a tray or serving platter. Sprinkle the Parmigiano and salt evenly over the pizza. Distribute the basil on top. Slice and serve immediately.

stracciatella pie

MAKES ONE 10- TO
12-INCH PIZZA • In Italian,
stracciatella means shreds.
As a cheese, it's a soft form
of mozzarella that melts
very quickly, becoming
molten almost instantly.
In Italy it's often used in
soups. With pizza, you'll
find that stracciatella placed
on the hot pie just out of
the oven turns the pizza
into a masterpiece that
looks like you slaved and
worried over it—when in
fact you surely didn't. It's
quick and easy—and in my
restaurant it is ordered so
often I sometimes think it's
all the guys in the back are
cooking.

1 ball of **Pizza Dough**,
shaped and waiting on a
floured peel (page 26)

70 grams (¼ cup) **Basic
Tomato Sauce** (page 34)

Generous pinch of **fine sea
salt**

Freshly ground **black pepper**

70 grams (about 2½ ounces)
stracciatella cheese

20 to 25 grams (about
¾ ounce) **arugula**

Extra-virgin olive oil, for
drizzling

1 Put the pizza stone on a rack in a gas oven about
8 inches from the broiler. Preheat the oven on bake at
500°F for 30 minutes. Switch to broil for 10 minutes.
(For an electric variation, see page 18.)

2 With the dough on the peel, spoon the tomato sauce
over the surface and spread it evenly, leaving about an
inch of the rim untouched. Sprinkle with salt and
pepper.

3 With quick, jerking motions, slide the pie onto the
stone. Broil for 3 minutes under gas (somewhat longer
with an electric oven; see page 18), until the top is
bubbling and the crust is nicely charred but not burnt.

4 Using the peel, transfer the pizza to a tray or serving
platter. Distribute the cheese in clumps over the
surface of the pie; it will melt and spread immediately.
Cover it with the arugula and drizzle with oil. Slice
and serve.

NOTE Stracciatella is not
in every cheese store,
even many of those with
an especially broad
selection. I buy ours
from Buon Italia in New
York City and it is on the
store's website. It's worth
ordering and waiting for.

amalfi pie

1 ball of **Pizza Dough**, shaped and waiting on a floured peel (page 26)

6 grams (about 1 fillet) **salt-packed anchovies** (see page 17), rinsed and dried

30 grams (about 6) pitted **green olives**

70 grams (¼ cup) **Basic Tomato Sauce** (page 34)

3 grams (1½ teaspoons) **chili flakes**

Extra-virgin olive oil, for drizzling

Coarsely chopped **parsley**, for garnish

MAKES ONE 10- TO 12-INCH PIZZA • The blazingly beautiful Amalfi Coast, near Naples, draws people for the scenery, for the startlingly gorgeous, sharply winding roads (they're not for the weak of stomach), and for the produce and seafood. The people are avid pizza eaters there, naturally enough, and—in their honor—I've created one with anchovies, olives, and chili flakes. This one is quite hot, about at the limit of spiciness for a pizza, but at the same time the flavor of the anchovies and olives manages to come through.

1 Put the pizza stone in a gas oven on a rack about 8 inches from the broiler. Preheat the oven on bake at 500°F for 30 minutes. Switch to broil for 10 minutes. (For an electric variation, see page 18.)

2 Finely chop the anchovies and olives together. Set aside.

3 With the dough on the peel, spoon the tomato sauce over the surface and spread it evenly, leaving about an inch of the rim untouched. Dollop the anchovy-olive mixture over the pizza. Sprinkle the chili flakes over the top and drizzle with olive oil.

4 With quick, jerking motions, slide the pie onto the stone. Broil for 3 minutes under gas (somewhat longer with an electric oven; see page 18), until the top is bubbling and the crust is nicely charred but not burnt.

5 Using the peel, transfer the pizza to a tray or serving platter before slicing it into wedges. Garnish with parsley. Serve immediately.

spicy eggplant pie

MAKES ONE 10- TO 12-INCH PIZZA • Still on a semivegetarian kick (the smoky bonito flakes being the intruder here), I came up with this pie. It's a good idea to broil the eggplant early, just to get it out of the way. Place the baking sheet on the stone while it preheats under the broiler. (When the eggplant goes on the pie to cook further, the steam from the other ingredients will keep it from burning.) I don't usually use as much chili pepper as I do in this recipe, but the way it plays against the delicate eggplant medallions is ideal. I offer a choice of hot peppers because the one that I prefer by far, the Thai chili, may be difficult to find.

200 grams (2 small) **Japanese eggplants**, cut into ¾-inch-thick rounds

1 ball of **Pizza Dough**, shaped and waiting on a floured peel (page 26)

70 grams (¼ cup) **Basic Tomato Sauce** (page 34)

8 grams (1¼ teaspoons) grated fresh **ginger**

1 medium **garlic clove**, chopped

4 grams (1 teaspoon) minced **chili pepper** (Thai, cayenne, or serrano)

Generous pinch of **fine sea salt**

6 **cilantro leaves**, torn

Extra-virgin olive oil, for drizzling

1 gram (1 tablespoon) dried aged **bonito flakes**

1   Put the pizza stone in a gas oven on a rack about 8 inches from the broiler. Preheat the oven on bake at 500°F for 30 minutes. Switch to broil for 10 minutes. (For an electric variation, see page 18.)

2   While the oven preheats, place the eggplant rounds on a baking sheet and broil for a couple of minutes, just until the tops are lightly browned. Set aside to cool.

3   With the dough on the peel, spoon the tomato sauce evenly over the surface, leaving about 1 inch of the rim untouched. Sprinkle the sauce with the ginger, garlic, chili pepper, and salt. Distribute the eggplant rounds over the surface.

4   With quick, jerking motions, slide the pie onto the stone. Broil for 3 to 3½ minutes under gas (somewhat longer with an electric oven; see page 18), until the top is bubbling and the crust is nicely charred but not burnt.

5   Using the peel, slide the pie onto a platter or serving tray. Distribute the cilantro on top, drizzle with oil, and sprinkle with the bonito flakes.

NOTE Bonito flakes are available at Asian specialty markets and online.

fennel and sausage pie

1 ball of **Pizza Dough**, shaped and waiting on a floured peel (page 26)

70 grams (¼ cup) **Basic Tomato Sauce** (page 34)

40 grams (about 1½ ounces) fresh **mozzarella**, pulled into 5 clumps

40 grams (scant ¼ cup) **Pork Sausage** (page 124)

50 grams (scant 1 cup) thinly sliced **fennel** (use a mandoline if available), a few fronds reserved for garnish

Extra-virgin olive oil, for drizzling

15 grams (⅛ cup) thinly sliced **onion**

Pinch of **fine sea salt**

Pinch of **chili flakes**

15 grams (¼ cup) finely grated **Parmigiano-Reggiano cheese**

MAKES ONE 10- TO 12-INCH PIZZA • When I'm not inventing things, having some fun, much of what I do—as you may have gathered by now—is really an homage to the great cooks of Italy. And those wonderful cooks do love their sausage and fennel. Here the pizza flatbread is my substitute for linguine.

1 Put the pizza stone in a gas oven on a rack about 8 inches from the broiler. Preheat the oven on bake at 500°F for 30 minutes. Switch to broil for 10 minutes. (For an electric variation, see page 18.)

2 With the dough on the peel, spoon the tomato sauce over the surface and spread it evenly, leaving about an inch of the rim untouched. Distribute the mozzarella and clumps of sausage over the pie. Cover with slices of fennel. Drizzle oil over the fennel, then spread the onion evenly over the top. Sprinkle with salt, chili flakes, and Parmigiano.

3 With quick, jerking motions, slide the pie onto the stone. Broil for 4½ minutes under gas (somewhat longer with an electric oven; see page 18), until the top is bubbling and the crust is nicely charred but not burnt. Garnish with fennel fronds.

4 Using the peel, transfer the pizza to a tray or serving platter before slicing it into wedges. Serve immediately.

giardiniera pie

MAKES ONE 10- TO
12-INCH PIZZA • The
giardiniera is another pizza,
of several in this book, where
the flatbread is garnished
with a spartan touch. For
one thing, it has no cheese
or meat—a purely vegetarian
pizza. But the mild raw
corn, the heat of the chili,
and natural spiciness of the
arugula all work to create
something that will make you
proud.

It's best, of course, if
you make this pizza in corn
season, when the kernels will
be sweetest.

1 ball of **Pizza Dough**,
shaped and waiting on a
floured peel (page 26)

80 grams (⅓ cup) **Basic
Tomato Sauce** (page 34)

Extra-virgin olive oil, for
drizzling

Generous pinch of **fine sea
salt**

3 grams (1½ teaspoons) **chili
flakes**

1 small **garlic clove**, sliced
paper-thin

90 grams (½ cup) fresh **corn
kernels**

28 grams (1 ounce) **arugula**

1 Put the pizza stone in a gas oven on a rack about
8 inches from the broiler. Preheat the oven on bake at
500°F for 30 minutes. Switch to broil for 10 minutes.
(For an electric variation, see page 18.)

2 With the dough on the peel, spoon the tomato sauce
over the surface and spread it evenly, leaving about an
inch of the rim untouched. Drizzle the oil over the pie.
Sprinkle the salt, chili flakes, and garlic evenly over
the top.

3 With quick, jerking motions, slide the pie onto the
stone. Broil for 3½ minutes under gas (somewhat
longer with an electric oven; see page 18), until the
top is bubbling and the crust is nicely charred but
not burnt.

4 Using the peel, transfer the pizza to a tray or serving
platter. Distribute the corn and arugula evenly over
the pie. Slice and serve immediately.

radicchio pie

MAKES ONE 10- TO
12-INCH PIZZA • These days
we're familiar with radicchio
mostly in its raw form as
a component of salads.
But in Italy it is frequently
grilled, the bitter spiciness
enhanced by the charring.
So, with that in mind, I knew
radicchio was a perfect
ingredient to adorn a pizza
cooked under the broiler.

1 ball of **Pizza Dough**,
shaped and waiting on a
floured peel (page 26)

80 grams (⅓ cup) **Basic
Tomato Sauce** (page 34)

60 grams (about 2 ounces)
Taleggio cheese, rind
removed, cut into 1-inch cubes

25 grams (about 6) pitted
Alfonso or **kalamata olives**,
halved

15 grams (1 tablespoon)
Caramelized Onions
(page 118)

70 grams **radicchio** (about
½ small head), sliced into
¼-inch strips

1 gram (about 1 teaspoon)
fresh **thyme leaves**

Extra-virgin olive oil, for
drizzling

1 Put the pizza stone in a gas oven on a rack about
8 inches from the broiler. Preheat the oven on bake at
500°F for 30 minutes. Switch to broil for 10 minutes.
(For an electric variation, see page 18.)

2 With the dough on the peel, spoon the tomato sauce
over the surface and spread it evenly, leaving about an
inch of the rim untouched. Distribute the cheese and
olives evenly over the sauce. Scatter the onions and
then the radicchio over the pie.

3 With quick, jerking motions, slide the pie onto the
stone. Broil for 3 to 3½ minutes under gas (somewhat
longer with an electric oven; see page 18), until the
top is bubbling and the crust is nicely charred but
not burnt.

4 Using the peel, transfer the pizza to a tray or serving
platter. Sprinkle with the thyme and drizzle with the
oil. Slice and serve immediately.

zucchini pie

110 grams (½ medium) **zucchini**

Fine sea salt

Pinch of finely grated **lemon zest**

1 ball of **Pizza Dough**, shaped and waiting on a floured peel (page 26)

70 grams (¼ cup) **Basic Tomato Sauce** (page 34)

70 grams (about 2¼ ounces) fresh **mozzarella**, pulled into 5 clumps

21 grams (about 3 fillets) **salt-packed anchovies** (see page 17), rinsed and dried

8 grams (about 1 tablespoon) drained **capers**

Pinch of **chili flakes**

3 medium **basil leaves**, torn

10 grams (about 3 tablespoons) finely grated **Parmigiano-Reggiano cheese**

MAKES ONE 10- TO 12-INCH PIZZA • I think of this as a summer pizza because that's when zucchini season reaches its height. But there are many other bright flavors playing with each other here. I think what will probably stand out for you is the anchovy-caper mix. This is a case where you definitely get a taste of the anchovy, which pretty much disappears in so many other preparations.

1 Put the pizza stone in a gas oven on a rack about 8 inches from the broiler. Preheat the oven on bake at 500°F for 30 minutes. Switch to broil for 10 minutes. (For an electric variation, see page 18.)

2 Slice the zucchini paper-thin, place in a small bowl, and toss with a sprinkling of salt and the lemon zest. Let macerate for about 20 minutes, until the zucchini releases its moisture. Pat dry and set aside.

3 With the dough on the peel, spoon the tomato sauce over the surface and spread it evenly, leaving about an inch of the rim untouched. Distribute the mozzarella over the pie.

4 Finely chop the anchovies and capers together. Dot the pie with the mix and arrange the zucchini slices artfully over the top. Sprinkle with the chili flakes.

5 With quick, jerking motions, slide the pie onto the stone. Broil for 3½ minutes under gas (somewhat longer with an electric oven; see page 18), until the top is bubbling and the crust is nicely charred but not burnt.

6 Using the peel, transfer the pizza to a tray or serving platter. Sprinkle the basil and Parmigiano over the pie. Slice and serve immediately.

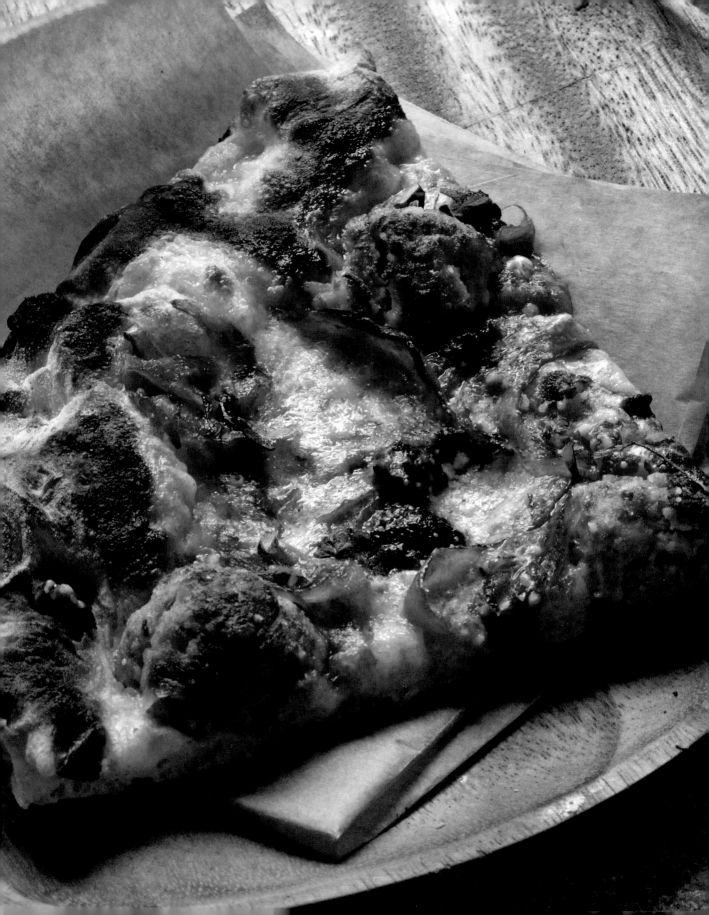

veal meatball pie

1 ball of **Pizza Dough**, shaped and waiting on a floured peel (page 26)

70 grams (¼ cup) **Basic Tomato Sauce** (page 34)

60 grams (about 2 ounces) fresh **mozzarella**, pulled into 5 clumps

4 or 5 **Veal Meatballs** (page 125), broken in half

12 grams (scant 1 tablespoon) **Caramelized Onions** (page 118)

20 grams (about 5) pitted **Alfonso olives**, halved

10 grams (about 3 tablespoons) grated **Parmigiano-Reggiano cheese**, plus more for serving

MAKES ONE 10- TO 12-INCH PIZZA • I know you have a picture in your mind about what this pizza will be, but the fresh veal meatballs, olives, onions, and cheese take it somewhere you may never have been before. That's why I just about always have it on the menu at the restaurant. People try it once and then, invariably, recommend it to friends.

1 Put the pizza stone in a gas oven on a rack about 8 inches from the broiler. Preheat the oven on bake at 500°F for 30 minutes. Switch to broil for 10 minutes. (For an electric variation, see page 18.)

2 With the dough on the peel, spoon the tomato sauce over the surface and spread it evenly, leaving about an inch of the rim untouched. Distribute the mozzarella over the sauce. Space the meatballs evenly over the pie. Distribute the onions evenly on top, then the olives. Sprinkle with the Parmigiano.

3 With quick, jerking motions, slide the pie onto the stone. Broil for 4½ minutes under gas (somewhat longer with an electric oven; see page 18), until the top is bubbling and the crust is nicely charred but not burnt.

4 Using the peel, transfer the pizza to a tray or serving platter. Sprinkle additional Parmigiano over the pie. Slice and serve immediately.

(recipe continues)

meatballs and tomato sauce

SERVES 4 OR 5 • When I top a pizza with meatballs, I break them into pieces and put them on the pie before it goes into the oven. But I serve them whole—minus the crust—as an appetizer, accompanied by a slightly more complex sauce than the one on the pie. Solo, they get a chance to shine, and I felt both grateful and flattered when *New York* magazine named them the best in the city. Serve the meatballs, generously sauced, with crusty bread and a green salad.

1 kilo (about 2 pounds) ripe **tomatoes**

150 grams (generous 1¼ cups) diced **onion**

75 grams (½ cup) diced **celery**

50 grams (about ⅓ cup) diced **carrot**

1 **bay leaf**

1 whole dried **chili pepper**

8 grams (1 teaspoon) **fine sea salt**

Veal Meatballs (page 125)

1 Bring a large pot of water to a boil. Plunge the tomatoes into the boiling water for 3 seconds. Remove them, peel, and, in a medium bowl, crush them to a pulp before passing through a sieve. Set aside, discarding anything left in the sieve.

2 In a large saucepan, combine the tomatoes, onion, celery, and carrot. Add the bay leaf, chili pepper, salt, and meatballs. Bring to a boil and continue to boil gently for 40 minutes. Remove the bay leaf and chili.

amatriciana pie

40 grams (¼ cup) diced **pancetta**

1 ball of **Pizza Dough**, shaped and waiting on a floured peel (page 26)

80 grams (⅓ cup) **Basic Tomato Sauce** (page 34)

40 grams (about 1½ ounces) **pecorino fresco** (see page 17), cut into 1-inch cubes

6 grams (about 2 very thin slices) **red onion**

Pinch of **chili flakes**

Generous pinch of **fine sea salt**

Extra-virgin olive oil, for drizzling

Chopped **parsley**, for garnish

MAKES ONE 10- TO 12-INCH PIZZA • Amatrice, a mountainous Italian town, became famous millennia ago for a tomato sauce–based pasta using pig cheek and sheep's-milk cheese (pecorino). It became a Roman classic, Amatriciana. I've never seen it as the basis for a pizza topping in Italy—but it does make sense as one. I use pancetta, from the belly, rather than the cheek meat, and keep the pie very basic.

1 Put the pizza stone in a gas oven on a rack about 8 inches from the broiler. Preheat the oven on bake at 500°F for 30 minutes. Switch to broil for 10 minutes. (For an electric variation, see page 18.)

2 Meanwhile, cook the pancetta in a small sauté pan over medium heat for 3 to 4 minutes, until browned lightly. Let cool.

3 With the dough on the peel, spoon the tomato sauce evenly over the surface, leaving about an inch of the rim untouched. Distribute the pecorino, pancetta, and onion over the sauce. Season with the chili flakes, salt, and oil.

4 With quick, jerking motions, slide the pie onto the stone. Broil for 3 to 3½ minutes under gas (somewhat longer with an electric oven; see page 18), until the top is bubbling and the crust is nicely charred but not burnt.

5 Using the peel, transfer the pizza to a tray or serving platter. Garnish with parsley. Slice and serve immediately.

boscaiola pie

MAKES ONE 10- TO 12-INCH PIZZA • The boscaiola is very familiar to Italians and travelers in Italy. More often than not, people order either it or a Margherita (page 41). I think I had my first one in Rome when I was in my early twenties. From the first taste, I must have seen how roasting enhances the flavor of mushrooms immeasurably, imparting enough personality to stand up to the spiciness of the chili flakes and the flavorful red onion and sausage.

1 ball of **Pizza Dough**, shaped and waiting on a floured peel (page 26)

70 grams (¼ cup) **Basic Tomato Sauce** (page 34)

50 grams (about ¼ cup) **Pork Sausage** (page 124)

40 grams (heaping ½ cup) thinly sliced **cremini mushrooms**

15 grams (about ⅛ cup) thinly sliced **red onion**, separated into ribbons

Pinch of **chili flakes**

Pinch of **fine sea salt**

1 Put the pizza stone in a gas oven on a rack about 8 inches from the broiler. Preheat the oven on bake at 500°F for 30 minutes. Switch to broil for 10 minutes. (For an electric variation, see page 18.)

2 With the dough on the peel, spoon the tomato sauce over the surface and spread it evenly, leaving about an inch of the rim untouched. Place the sausage in small mounds around the pizza. Distribute the mushrooms and onion evenly on top. Sprinkle evenly with the chili flakes and salt.

3 With quick, jerking motions, slide the pie onto the stone. Broil for 3½ to 4 minutes under gas (somewhat longer with an electric oven; see page 18), until the top is bubbling and the crust is nicely charred but not burnt.

4 Using the peel, transfer the pizza to a tray or serving platter. Slice into wedges and serve immediately.

pepperoni pie

1 ball of **Pizza Dough**, shaped and waiting on a floured peel (page 26)

80 grams (⅓ cup) **Red Pepper Sauce** (page 127)

30 grams (about 1 ounce) **pecorino fresco** (see page 17), cut into ½-inch cubes

50 grams (¼ cup) **Merguez** (page 123)

Pinch of **chili flakes**

4 grams (about 1 very thin slice) **red onion**

6 to 8 **mint leaves** for garnish

1 Put the pizza stone in a gas oven on a rack about 8 inches from the broiler. Preheat the oven on bake at 500°F for 30 minutes. Switch to broil for 10 minutes. (For an electric variation, see page 18.)

2 With the dough on the peel, spoon the pepper sauce over the surface and spread it evenly, leaving about an inch of the rim untouched. Distribute the pecorino fresco and clumps of sausage evenly over the pie. Season with the chili flakes and scatter the onion.

3 With quick, jerking motions, slide the pie onto the stone. Broil for 3½ to 4 minutes under gas (somewhat longer with an electric oven; see page 18), until the top is bubbling and the crust is nicely charred but not burnt.

4 Using the peel, transfer the pizza to a tray or serving platter before slicing it into wedges. Garnish with mint. Serve immediately.

MAKES ONE 10- TO 12-INCH PIZZA • Right off I have to tell you there's no pepperoni sausage on this pie—a fact that has caused servers at the restaurant untold moments of awkwardness—but the title is accurate nevertheless: The word is the Italian plural for *pepper*. And peppers make this pie. Pureed, red peppers become a sauce that's sweet but complex. This pie is, in fact, adorned with dollops of sausage, but it's merguez here, a lamb sausage that's a fixture of North African cuisine, and a natural pairing for the peppers.

Starter White Pie

WHITE SAUCE PIZZAS

béchamel sauce 66

starter white pie 67

flambé pie 68

ham and peas pie 71

leek and sausage pie 72

charcuterie pie 75

honshimeji and guanciale pie 76

cauliflower pie 79

three-mushroom pie 80

corn and tomato pie 83

onion pie 84

coppa and fennel pie 86

potato and leek pie 87

brussels sprouts and chestnut pie 89

broccoli rabe pie 90

Often, when I make a pizza, I'm looking for something less assertive, something more neutral than tomatoes—and yet more than a bare crust—to create the base for the pie. That's where a béchamel sauce can be brilliant. It binds the toppings in a velvety smoothness, without the acidic sweetness that tomato adds. Many of my pizzas rely on this fundamental white sauce—a sauce that you're probably more accustomed to seeing in classic Italian dishes like lasagna, as well as a great deal of French cooking (the French manage to frenchify it, of course, sanctifying it as one of the five "mother sauces").

béchamel sauce

MAKES 470 GRAMS (ABOUT 2 CUPS); OR ENOUGH FOR ABOUT 8 PIZZAS • A standard way to prepare béchamel is to cook the flour and butter first and then add the milk. But there are other approaches. I prefer the one here—simmering some milk and butter to begin the sauce rather than cooking the butter and flour to start—partly because it's the method I was originally taught, but also because I find it faster and foolproof. The result is reliably light in texture and color.

486 grams (2 cups) **whole milk**

113 grams (1 stick) **unsalted butter**

18 grams (about 2¼ tablespoons) **all-purpose flour**

2 grams (¼ teaspoon) **fine sea salt**

3 rasp grates of **nutmeg** or a pinch of ground nutmeg

1 Pour about one-third of the milk into a saucepan. Cut the butter into a few chunks (so they'll melt more easily) and add to the milk. Heat over medium-low heat, stirring, until the butter melts but without allowing the milk to reach a boil.

2 Meanwhile, put the flour in a medium mixing bowl, add the remaining milk, and whisk into a slurry. Once the butter has been completely incorporated into the hot milk, ladle some of the warm mixture into the cold flour mixture to warm it. Pour the contents of the bowl back into the saucepan and whisk it in. Stir in the salt.

3 Over medium-low heat, whisk the mixture frequently—to prevent sticking—as it cooks and thickens. The béchamel is done at about 180°F, when it has reached the consistency of a runny sauce or heavy cream. Grate in the nutmeg and allow the sauce to cool to room temperature. It will continue to thicken slightly as it cools. Use the béchamel immediately or cool, cover, and refrigerate for up to 5 days; bring it back to room temperature before using.

starter white pie

1 ball of **Pizza Dough**, shaped and waiting on a floured peel (page 26)

60 grams (¼ cup) **Béchamel** (page 66)

15 grams (¼ cup) finely grated **Parmigiano-Reggiano cheese**

40 grams (about 1½ ounces) fresh **mozzarella**, pulled into 5 clumps

Pinch of **fine sea salt**

6 fresh **rosemary leaves**

1 Put the pizza stone in a gas oven on a rack about 8 inches from the broiler. Preheat the oven on bake at 500°F for 30 minutes. Switch to broil for 10 minutes. (For an electric variation, see page 18.)

2 With the dough on the peel, spoon the béchamel over the surface and spread it evenly, leaving about an inch of the rim untouched. Sprinkle the surface with the Parmigiano. Distribute the clumps of mozzarella. Sprinkle with salt and strategically place the rosemary.

3 With quick, jerking motions, slide the pie onto the stone. Broil for about 3 minutes under gas (somewhat longer with an electric oven; see page 18). The ingredients should be bubbling and the crust nicely charred but not burnt.

4 Using the peel, transfer the pizza to a tray or serving platter before slicing it into wedges. Serve immediately.

MAKES ONE 10- TO 12-INCH PIZZA • This very fundamental béchamel-based pizza highlights the beauty and malleability of the sauce, and also provides the Parmesan and rosemary that I pair with it a rare chance to show their stuff, without a lot of competition from other ingredients. I call it a starter pizza because it may well be the most basic, efficient way to start trying the pizzas in this book. For this one you can concentrate on preparing your first crust and not have to think about much more than that. (The first two or three pies in the red sauce section serve a similar introductory purpose.)

flambé pie

MAKES ONE 10- TO 12-INCH PIZZA • I had my first tarte flambé, an Alsatian pizza, about twenty years ago in Paris, and the smoky-rich flavors never left my mind. The main ingredients are crème fraîche, onions, and bacon on a crusty bread. The combination has an elemental sense to it; like so much of what I lean toward, it's a bit primitive—satisfying working-class food. When I opened Co., I reached into my memory bank and pulled out ideas that resonated with that first taste. I decided to switch away from crème fraîche to a glossy béchamel and use it as the foundation for the ingredients, instead of spreading it on top of them as the French do. I caramelize the onions to force out their sweetness and opt for diced smoky bacon, distributed with a bit of flair.

1 ball of **Pizza Dough**, shaped and waiting on a floured peel (page 26)

45 grams (3 tablespoons) **Béchamel** (page 66)

15 grams (¼ cup) finely grated **Parmigiano-Reggiano cheese**

40 grams (about 1½ ounces) fresh **mozzarella**, pulled into 5 clumps

70 grams (about 10) **Lardons** (page 122)

50 grams (¼ cup) **Caramelized Onions** (page 118)

Pinch of **fine sea salt**

1 Put the pizza stone in a gas oven on a rack about 8 inches from the broiler. Preheat the oven on bake at 500°F for 30 minutes. Switch to broil for 10 minutes. (For an electric variation, see page 18.)

2 With the dough on the peel, spoon the béchamel over the surface and spread it evenly, leaving about an inch of the rim untouched. Sprinkle with the Parmigiano and distribute the mozzarella over the top. Place lardons between the clumps of cheese. Distribute the onions over everything, then sprinkle with salt.

3 With quick, jerking motions, slide the pie onto the stone. Broil for 3 to 3½ minutes under gas (somewhat longer with an electric oven; see page 18). The pie should be bubbling and the crust well charred but not burnt.

4 Using the peel, transfer the pizza to a tray or serving platter before slicing it into wedges. Serve immediately.

ham and peas pie

1 ball of **Pizza Dough**, shaped and waiting on a floured peel (page 26)

60 grams (¼ cup) **Béchamel** (page 66)

15 grams (¼ cup) finely grated **Parmigiano-Reggiano** or **Grana Padano cheese**

40 grams (about 1½ ounces) fresh **mozzarella**, pulled into 5 clumps

60 grams (about 2 ounces) sliced **prosciutto**, ripped into shreds

25 to 30 grams (about 1 ounce or scant ¼ cup) fresh **peas** (or defrosted frozen, patted dry)

5 grams (2 to 3 large) fresh **mint leaves**, thinly sliced

MAKES ONE 10- TO 12-INCH PIZZA • In Italy, ham, peas, and cream are often combined in a smooth dressing for pasta. It didn't take much for it to dawn on me that something similar, if a bit more complex, would make a fine pizza. (I often think of pasta when I'm trying to come up with a new pizza.) The finished pie, thanks in part to the uncooked mint added at the end, has a home-garden, vegetal flavor that leaves you feeling refreshed.

1 Put the pizza stone in a gas oven on a rack about 8 inches from the broiler. Preheat the oven on bake at 500°F for 30 minutes. Switch to broil for 10 minutes. (For an electric variation, see page 18.)

2 With the dough on the peel, spoon the béchamel over the surface and spread it evenly, leaving about an inch of the rim untouched. Sprinkle the surface with the Parmigiano. Distribute the mozzarella and prosciutto over the top. Sprinkle the peas over all.

3 With quick, jerking motions, slide the pie onto the stone. Broil for 3 to 3½ minutes under gas (somewhat longer with an electric oven; see page 18), until the top is bubbling and the crust is nicely charred but not burnt.

4 Using the peel, transfer the pizza to a tray or serving platter. Distribute the mint over the top. Slice and serve immediately.

leek and sausage pie

MAKES ONE 10- TO 12-INCH PIZZA • Sausage and onions make a dynamite combination that we all know well. But here, instead of onions, I use the sweeter leek as the foil for spicy sausage meat, and place it over a soft preparation of béchamel and cheeses. The invention is based on a familiar version of lasagna. In essence, I've taken one of the world's great comfort foods as my starting point but turned to good bread as the carrier of the flavors. This pizza cooks longer than many of the others because the ingredients are heavier and require more time. It's still fast, once you're ready to go.

65 grams (1 small) **leek**

24 grams (1 tablespoon) **sea salt**

1 ball of **Pizza Dough**, shaped and waiting on a floured peel (page 26)

45 grams (3 tablespoons) **Béchamel** (page 66)

15 grams (¼ cup) finely grated **Parmigiano-Reggiano** or **Grana Padano cheese**

40 grams (about 1½ ounces) fresh **mozzarella**, pulled into 5 clumps

65 grams (scant ⅓ cup) **Pork Sausage** (page 124)

7 to 8 grams (1 heaping tablespoon) fresh **bread crumbs**

Pinch of **chili flakes**

1 Put the pizza stone in a gas oven on a rack about 8 inches from the broiler. Preheat the oven on bake at 500°F for 30 minutes. Switch to broil for 10 minutes. (For an electric variation, see page 18.)

2 Remove the leek's tough outer leaves. Slice away the root end carefully so the rest of the leek remains intact. Cut away most of the deep green top of the leek, leaving an inch or two of pale green above the white part. Cut the leek almost in half lengthwise, being careful not to slice through the base, so the leek keeps its shape. Wash the individual leaves under running water until they are free of dirt and grit.

3 Choose a saucepan just large enough to hold the leek. Nearly fill the pan with water, add the salt, and bring to a boil. Place the leek in the pan, lower the heat, and simmer until tender, about 5 minutes. Remove the leek and set aside to cool to room temperature.

4 With the dough on the peel, spoon the béchamel over the surface and spread it evenly, leaving about an inch of the rim untouched. Sprinkle the surface with the Parmigiano. Distribute the clumps of mozzarella. Separate the leaves from the leek and distribute them over the pie. Space 5 or 6 clumps of sausage meat, about a tablespoon each, over the pie. Sprinkle evenly with the bread crumbs and chili flakes.

With quick, jerking motions, slide the pie onto the stone. Broil for 4½ minutes under gas (somewhat longer with an electric oven; see page 18), until the top is bubbling and the crust is nicely charred but not burnt.

6 Using the peel, transfer the pizza to a tray or serving platter. Slice into wedges and serve immediately.

charcuterie pie

1 ball of **Pizza Dough**, shaped and waiting on a floured peel (page 26)

60 grams (¼ cup) **Béchamel** (page 66)

15 grams (¼ cup) finely grated **Parmigiano-Reggiano** or **Grana Padano cheese**

40 grams (about 1½ ounces) fresh **mozzarella**, pulled into 5 clumps

80 to 100 grams (½ to ¾ cup) **sauerkraut**, squeezed of excess liquid

40 grams (about ½) **knockwurst sausage**

40 grams (about ½) **bratwurst sausage**

15 to 20 grams (2 to 3 teaspoons) **Dijon mustard**

1 Put the pizza stone in a gas oven on a rack about 8 inches from the broiler. Preheat the oven on bake at 500°F for 30 minutes. Switch to broil for 10 minutes. (For an electric variation, see page 18.)

2 With the dough on the peel, spoon the béchamel over the surface and spread it evenly, leaving about an inch of the rim untouched. Sprinkle the surface with the Parmigiano. Distribute the mozzarella and the sauerkraut over the top. Slice the sausages in half lengthwise, then cut them into 1-inch pieces. Place the sausage pieces evenly over the pie.

3 With quick, jerking motions, slide the pie onto the stone. Broil for 4 minutes under gas (somewhat longer with an electric oven; see page 18), until the top is bubbling and the crust is nicely charred but not burnt.

4 Using the peel, transfer the pizza to a tray or serving platter. Dab or drizzle the mustard over the top. Slice and serve immediately.

MAKES ONE 10- TO 12-INCH PIZZA • Every now and then when I was creating this pie, I would break out into a chorus of "Take me out to the ballgame, take me out to the crowd. . . ." The reason, of course, is that this is my pizza version of a hot dog on a bun (in fact, you could substitute good beef franks for the sausages). It's all about being whimsical, making people laugh, but still reaching the flavor and quality standard I strive for. The reason everybody loves a hot dog is that it's a terrific combination of salt, beef, fermented cabbage, and a bite of mustard, all encased in bread. Here, I hope you'll agree, the crisp pizza base is better than a doughy bun, and broiling the sauerkraut provides an additional burst of flavor.

honshimeji and guanciale pie

MAKES ONE 10- TO 12-INCH PIZZA • The two featured players in this pizza are both singularly fascinating stars in the culinary firmament. The honshimeji is an Asian mushroom with a small head. It can be brown or white, and can be found in just about every store that boasts a wide selection of mushrooms. It's too bitter to eat raw; cooked, it turns into pure sweetness. As for the guanciale, if you didn't know better you'd think it was bacon (and, in fact, feel free to substitute that if the mood—or convenience—moves you), but it's a cut from the jowl of the pig, not the loin, which is where most bacon comes from. And even though it's cured and presents an assertive flavor, it's not smoked as bacon often is. This ingredient combination makes for a crunchy, strong-flavored pizza. For an herbal accent, I've added, judiciously, a few leaves of rosemary.

1 ball of **Pizza Dough**, shaped and waiting on a floured peel (page 26)

60 grams (¼ cup) **Béchamel** (page 66)

50 grams (about 1¾ ounces) fresh **mozzarella**, pulled into 5 clumps

About 10 fresh **rosemary leaves**

½ **garlic clove**, finely chopped

55 grams (2 ounces) **honshimeji mushrooms**, separated from the larger cluster

15 grams (5 or 6 thin slices) **guanciale** (or bacon)

4 **quail eggs** (or the smallest eggs you can find)

1 Put the pizza stone in a gas oven on a rack about 8 inches from the broiler. Preheat the oven on bake at 500°F for 30 minutes. Switch to broil for 10 minutes. (For an electric variation, see page 18.)

2 With the dough on the peel, spoon the béchamel over the surface and spread it evenly, leaving about an inch of the rim untouched. Distribute the clumps of mozzarella and sprinkle the rosemary and garlic evenly over the pie. Distribute the mushrooms, then top with a layer of the guanciale.

3 With quick, jerking motions, slide the pie onto the stone. Broil under gas for 2½ to 3 minutes (somewhat longer with an electric oven; see page 18).

4 Using the peel, remove the pizza. Close the oven to retain heat.

5 Crack the eggs open gently so the yolks stay whole. Slip them out of their shells and space the eggs evenly around the pizza. Return the pie to the oven to broil for about 1 minute more, until the crust is nicely charred and the eggs are just set.

6 Using the peel, transfer the pizza to a tray or serving platter. Slice the pizza into wedges, bursting the yolks so they spread a bit. Serve immediately.

cauliflower pie

150 grams (1½ cups) **cauliflower florets**

1 ball of **Pizza Dough**, shaped and waiting on a floured peel (page 26)

60 grams (¼ cup) **Béchamel** (page 66)

10 grams (3 tablespoons) finely grated **Parmigiano-Reggiano** or **Grana Padano cheese**

50 grams (about 1¾ ounces) **mozzarella**, pulled into 5 clumps

15 grams (1½ tablespoons) coarsely chopped **green olives**

½ **garlic clove**, finely chopped

Generous pinch of **chili flakes**

10 grams (1½ tablespoons) fresh **bread crumbs**

Chopped **fresh parsley** for sprinkling

MAKES ONE 10- TO 12-INCH PIZZA • Cauliflower may strike you as lacking in sufficient character for a pizza, but roasting it is going to draw out the flavor you might not have known it had. Roasting will also give it texture (the roasting process removes about half of its natural liquid). Then you go on to combine it with powerhouses like olives, garlic, and chili and, trust me, you can forget the word *bland*.

1 Place a pizza stone in a gas oven about 8 inches from the broiler. Preheat the oven to 500°F for 30 minutes. (For an electric variation, see page 18.)

2 Crumble the cauliflower with your fingers and spread it evenly in an 8-inch pie pan or baking dish. Set the pan on the pizza stone and roast the cauliflower for 12 minutes, until it is flecked with char and slightly translucent, then remove it and set aside. Switch to broil and continue to heat the stone for another 10 minutes.

3 With the dough on the peel, spoon the béchamel over the surface and spread it evenly, leaving about an inch of the rim untouched. Sprinkle the surface with the Parmigiano. Distribute the mozzarella, the cauliflower pieces, and then the olives, garlic, and chili flakes evenly over the pizza. Sprinkle the bread crumbs over the top.

4 With quick, jerking motions, slide the pie onto the stone. Broil for 3 to 3½ minutes under gas (somewhat longer with an electric oven; see page 18), until the top is bubbling and the crust is nicely charred but not burnt.

5 Using the peel, transfer the pizza to a tray or serving platter. Sprinkle parsley over the top. Slice and serve.

three-mushroom pie

MAKES ONE 10- TO 12-INCH PIZZA • Why the three mushrooms? Wouldn't one kind do? Well, yes. But then you'd miss out on a significant amount of visual and textural interest. This is a pizza that plays all its notes like a small orchestra. The mushrooms are mild and earthy; the garlic is cooked in oil (confit) to mellow it. Now add jalapeños to the toppings and they leap out of all that gentleness with a shot of heat. And, finally, there's the dill, which is neither hot nor mild, an herbaceous bridge between the two extremes.

1 ball of **Pizza Dough**, shaped and waiting on a floured peel (page 26)

60 grams (¼ cup) **Béchamel** (page 66)

15 grams (about ¼ cup) finely grated **Gruyère cheese**

20 grams (⅓ cup) finely grated **Pecorino Romano cheese**

Garlic Confit (recipe follows), coarsely chopped

80 grams (about 2¾ ounces) mixed **mushrooms** (such as chanterelles, shiitake caps, and oyster), cleaned and sliced

10 grams (¼ small) **jalapeño pepper**, halved lengthwise, seeded, and sliced paper-thin

4 grams (about ¾ teaspoon) **extra-virgin olive oil**

Pinch of **fine sea salt**

Fresh **dill**, for garnish

1 Put the pizza stone in a gas oven on a rack about 8 inches from the broiler. Preheat the oven on bake at 500°F for 30 minutes. Switch to broil for 10 minutes. (For an electric variation, see page 18.)

2 With the dough on the peel, spoon the béchamel over the surface and spread it evenly, leaving about an inch of the rim untouched. Sprinkle the sauce evenly with the Gruyère and then the pecorino. Arrange the garlic evenly over the pie, then distribute the mushrooms, jalapeño, oil, and salt.

3 With quick, jerking motions, slide the pie onto the stone. Broil for 3½ to 4 minutes under gas (somewhat longer with an electric oven; see page 18), until the top is bubbling and the crust is nicely charred but not burnt.

4 Using the peel, transfer the pizza to a tray or serving platter. Sprinkle generously with the tender ends of the dill sprigs. Slice and serve immediately.

garlic confit

MAKES 8 CLOVES

48 grams (8 large) peeled **garlic cloves**

140 grams (⅔ cup) **extra-virgin olive oil**

8 grams (1 teaspoon) **fine sea salt**

Combine the garlic, oil, and salt in a heavy saucepan. Bring to a simmer and cook until the garlic is tender, about 15 minutes. Drain well.

corn and tomato pie

1 ball of **Pizza Dough**, shaped and waiting on a floured peel (page 26)

60 grams (¼ cup) **Béchamel** (page 66)

10 grams (about 3 tablespoons) finely grated **Parmigiano-Reggiano cheese**

60 grams (about 2 ounces) fresh **mozzarella**, pulled into 5 clumps

1 medium **garlic clove**, finely chopped

Pinch of **chili flakes**

Fine sea salt

Extra-virgin olive oil, for drizzling

50 grams (4 to 6) **cherry tomatoes**, halved

60 grams (about ⅓ cup) fresh **corn kernels**

8 medium **basil leaves**, roughly torn

MAKES ONE 10- TO 12-INCH PIZZA • It was well into a recent summer before I got this pie right. At first, I was too eager and made do with early corn—but it just hadn't reached its potential yet. The corn has to be supremely juicy and sweet. I like the kernels to be so full they squirt when you scrape them (you should be able to hear the sound of the squirting even from a distance). If it's too early, before the corn has reached its full-flavored glory, you'll find your palate searching around for corn flavor, the very key to the composition.

1 Put the pizza stone in a gas oven on a rack about 8 inches from the broiler. Preheat the oven on bake at 500°F for 30 minutes. Switch to broil for 10 minutes. (For an electric variation, see page 18.)

2 With the dough on the peel, spoon the béchamel over the surface and spread it evenly, leaving about an inch of the rim untouched. Sprinkle the surface with the Parmigiano and distribute the mozzarella. Evenly sprinkle the pie with the garlic, chili flakes, and salt and drizzle just a little olive oil over the top. Arrange the tomato pieces over the pie and scatter the corn on top. Distribute the basil around the pie.

3 With quick, jerking motions, slide the pie onto the stone. Broil for 3½ minutes (somewhat longer with an electric oven; see page 18), until the top is bubbling and the crust is nicely charred but not burnt.

4 Using the peel, transfer the pizza to a tray or serving platter before slicing it into wedges. Serve immediately.

onion pie

MAKES ONE 10- TO 12-INCH PIZZA • I call this an onion pie because onions are at the heart of the creamy sauce that you'll prepare just before starting the rest of the pizza. The onion's milder cousins in the allium family, leeks and scallions, dominate the topping. In the end, this allium display is pale and soft against the crunch and char of the flatbread that presents it.

Fine sea salt

35 grams (½ small) **leek**, white part only, thinly sliced

1 ball of **Pizza Dough**, shaped and waiting on a floured peel (page 26)

60 grams (¼ cup) **Creamy Onion Sauce** (recipe follows)

30 grams (about 1 ounce) fresh **mozzarella**, pulled into 5 clumps

20 grams (about ⅓ cup) finely grated **Gruyère cheese**

70 grams (7 medium) **scallions**, white parts thinly sliced, green tops cut into 2-inch strips

Pinch of fresh chopped **rosemary leaves**

Freshly ground **black pepper**

1 Put the pizza stone in a gas oven on a rack about 8 inches from the broiler. Preheat the oven on bake at 500°F for 30 minutes. Switch to broil for 10 minutes. (For an electric variation, see page 18.)

2 Bring a small saucepan of salted water to a boil. Add the leek slices and blanch until tender, 2 to 3 minutes. Drain, pat dry, and set aside.

3 With the dough on the peel, spoon the onion sauce over the surface and spread it evenly, leaving about an inch of the rim untouched. Distribute the mozzarella and Gruyère around the pie. Scatter the leek and scallions on top. Sprinkle the pie with rosemary and black pepper.

4 With quick, jerking motions, slide the pie onto the stone. Broil for 4 minutes under gas (somewhat longer with an electric oven; see page 18), until the top is bubbling and the crust is nicely charred but not burnt.

5 Using the peel, transfer the pizza to a tray or serving platter before slicing it into wedges. Serve immediately.

creamy onion sauce

MAKES 460 GRAMS (1½ CUPS), OR ENOUGH FOR 5 PIES

200 grams (about 1 cup) **Caramelized Onions** (page 118)

250 grams (generous 1 cup) **heavy cream**

4 grams (1 teaspoon) finely grated **lemon zest**

4 grams (½ teaspoon) **fine sea salt**

1 Put the onions and cream in a saucepan over medium heat. Cook, stirring occasionally, until reduced by half, 15 to 20 minutes. Stir in the zest and salt.

2 Transfer the mixture to a blender or food processor and blend until smooth. Cool to room temperature.

coppa and fennel pie

MAKES ONE 10- TO 12-INCH PIZZA • Coppa, a salt- and spice-cured cut from the neck of the pig that is dried for months in a casing, is often compared to bresaola, dried beef. It's also not unlike prosciutto, which comes from the leg, but it is fattier, richer, and often sweeter. It stands up to the cooking in this recipe, where the more delicate prosciutto would not survive as well (which is why I tend to leave prosciutto uncooked, topping a pizza with it once the pie is baked).

1 ball of **Pizza Dough**, shaped and waiting on a floured peel (page 26)

60 grams (¼ cup) **Béchamel** (page 66)

15 grams (¼ cup) finely grated **Parmigiano-Reggiano cheese**

50 grams (about 1¾ ounces) fresh **mozzarella**, pulled into 5 clumps

60 grams (about 1 cup) shaved **fennel** (use a mandoline, if you have one), a few fronds reserved for garnish

30 grams (5 or 6 thin slices) **coppa**

Freshly ground **black pepper**

Grated zest of ¼ **lemon**

1 Put the pizza stone in a gas oven on a rack about 8 inches from the broiler. Preheat the oven on bake at 500°F for 30 minutes. Switch to broil for 10 minutes. (For an electric variation, see page 18.)

2 With the dough on the peel, spoon the béchamel over the surface and spread it evenly, leaving about an inch of the rim untouched. Sprinkle with the Parmigiano and distribute the mozzarella. Evenly distribute the shaved fennel and then the coppa over the pie.

3 With quick, jerking motions, slide the pie onto the stone. Broil for 3 to 3½ minutes under gas (somewhat longer with an electric oven; see page 18), until the top is bubbling and the crust is nicely charred but not burnt.

4 Using the peel, transfer the pizza to a tray or serving platter. Sprinkle with pepper, the zest, and then fennel fronds for color. Slice into wedges and serve immediately.

potato and leek pie

100 grams (1 small) **Yukon gold potato**, peeled and sliced paper-thin

Fine sea salt

120 grams (1¼ cups) chopped **leeks**, white part only

1 ball of **Pizza Dough**, shaped and waiting on a floured peel (page 26)

40 grams (about 2½ table-spoons) **Béchamel** (page 66)

40 grams (⅔ cup) finely grated **Gruyère cheese**

Leaves from 1 **rosemary sprig**

Freshly ground **black pepper**

Extra-virgin olive oil, for drizzling

MAKES ONE 10- TO 12-INCH PIZZA • In a very loose sense, what we have here is the vichyssoise of pizza. The basic potato and leek combination is brought into play, but there's an ingredient difference that, if you've already cooked a few of these pizzas, will strike you immediately: Béchamel plays the role on the crust that cream would play in the soup (although the pie requires less sauce than other pizzas because of the added moisture from the vegetables). In the end, the potatoes are going to be crispy, almost potato chips, as they top one of the most entertaining pizzas in the book.

1 Put the pizza stone in a gas oven on a rack about 8 inches from the broiler. Preheat the oven on bake at 500°F for 30 minutes. Switch to broil for 10 minutes. (For an electric variation, see page 18.)

2 Place the potato slices in a small saucepan with generously salted cold water. Bring the water to a boil, then drain the potatoes and set aside to cool.

3 Bring a small saucepan of salted water to a boil. Add the chopped leeks and blanch until tender, 2 to 3 minutes. Drain, pat dry, and set aside.

4 With the dough on the peel, spoon the béchamel over the surface and spread it evenly, leaving about an inch of the rim untouched. Combine the potatoes, leeks, Gruyère, rosemary, and pepper, along with a drizzle of oil, in a medium bowl and toss to evenly coat the potatoes.

5 Distribute the potato mixture evenly over the dough. Drizzle with a bit more oil. Broil for 4 minutes under gas (somewhat longer with an electric oven; see page 18), until the potatoes are crisp and the crust is blistered with a nice char.

6 Using the peel, transfer the pizza to a tray or serving platter, slice into wedges, and serve immediately.

NOTE The chestnuts in this recipe are roasted. It is a simple matter, especially in New York City, to buy them already roasted; you bump into chestnut carts all over Midtown in the wintertime. You can find them frozen, too, which is a lesser alternative, but acceptable (defrost them, then dry thoroughly). But if you are starting with fresh whole chestnuts, here's what to do: Preheat the oven to 350°F. Score the husk of each chestnut to let out the steam as they cook (the conventional way is to slice an X or a cross in the husk; a simpler technique is to just cut a gash into the shell). Put them in a roasting pan and roast until they split, about 30 minutes. As soon as they're cool enough to handle, peel off the husk. This is most easily accomplished when the chestnuts are still very warm.

brussels sprouts and chestnut pie

1 ball of **Pizza Dough**, shaped and waiting on a floured peel (page 26)

60 grams (¼ cup) **Béchamel** (page 66)

10 grams (about 3 tablespoons) finely grated **Parmigiano-Reggiano cheese**

40 grams (about 1½ ounces) fresh **mozzarella**, pulled into 5 clumps

45 grams (5 or 6 pieces) **Lardons** (page 122)

60 grams (1 cup) very thinly sliced **Brussels sprouts**

30 grams (about 8) peeled **roasted chestnuts**, sliced ⅛ inch thick (see Note)

10 grams (about ⅛ cup) thinly sliced **red onion**, separated into rings

Pinch of **chili flakes**

Celery salt

Extra-virgin olive oil, for drizzling

Leaves from 2 **thyme sprigs**

MAKES ONE 10- TO 12-INCH PIZZA • I have a soft spot for chestnuts because I remember so vividly the days when I picked them in Tuscany, the days when I was still a young man learning to cook and bake from my Italian friends on a farm there. But, even without that affectionate memory, I probably would have devised this pizza on some chilly day in early winter. A little brisk weather and, right away, I'm thinking Brussels sprouts—and then chestnuts pop into my mind. The sweet starchiness of chestnuts was made for the bitter, mustardy sprouts. The béchamel, as it usually does, softens and binds the toppings with its velvety underlying notes.

1 Put the pizza stone in a gas oven on a rack about 8 inches from the broiler. Preheat the oven on bake at 500°F for 30 minutes. Switch to broil for 10 minutes. (For an electric variation, see page 18.)

2 With the dough on the peel, spoon the béchamel over the surface and spread it evenly, leaving about an inch of the rim untouched. Sprinkle the sauce with the Parmigiano. Arrange the mozzarella and lardons on top. Distribute the Brussels sprouts, chestnuts, and onions, covering the pie, then sprinkle with the chili flakes and celery salt. Drizzle with some oil.

3 With quick, jerking motions, slide the pie onto the stone. Broil for 3 to 3½ minutes (somewhat longer with an electric oven; see page 18), until the top is bubbling and the crust is nicely charred.

4 Using the peel, transfer the pizza to a tray or serving platter. Sprinkle with the thyme leaves. Slice and serve immediately.

broccoli rabe pie

MAKES ONE 10- TO
12-INCH PIZZA • If you've
already made the Popeye—
my spinach pizza—this one
is going to seem somewhat
similar. But broccoli rabe
gives you a completely
different flavor, more
assertive, and offers more
resistance than spinach
does.

Fine sea salt

120 grams (about 5 stalks) **broccoli rabe**, tough ends trimmed, coarsely chopped

1 ball of **Pizza Dough**, shaped and waiting on a floured peel (page 26)

60 grams (¼ cup) **Béchamel** (page 66)

1 medium **garlic clove**, chopped

30 grams (about 1 ounce) **provolone**, shredded

40 grams (about 1½ ounces) fresh **mozzarella**, pulled into 5 clumps

2 grams (¼ teaspoon) chopped **Thai pepper**

1 Put the pizza stone in a gas oven on a rack about 8 inches from the broiler. Preheat the oven on bake at 500°F for 30 minutes. Switch to broil for 10 minutes. (For an electric variation, see page 18.)

2 Bring a medium pot of salted water to a simmer. Add the broccoli rabe and blanch for 10 seconds. Drain and set aside.

3 With the dough on the peel, spread the béchamel evenly over the surface, leaving about an inch of the rim untouched. Sprinkle with the garlic and provolone. Evenly space the clumps of mozzarella on top. Cover with a blanket of broccoli rabe and sprinkle with the Thai pepper and a pinch of salt.

4 With quick, jerking motions, slide the pie onto the stone. Broil for 3½ minutes (somewhat longer with an electric oven; see page 18), until the top is bubbling and the crust is nicely charred but not burnt.

5 Using the peel, transfer the pizza to a tray or serving platter before slicing it into wedges. Serve immediately.

NO SAUCE PIZZAS

Shiitake with Walnut Puree Pie

Dispensing with the usual sauce, whether red or white, may seem like a kind of pizza craziness, forcing the pizza to fend for itself half naked. But in some cases, that's an advantage, resulting in a pie that's clean in flavor and entirely reliant on the crust and the individual ingredients to speak on their own. More often than not, the sauce is essential; but when it's not, when its absence is a plus, you'll be delighted by the results.

bird's nest pie

120 grams (3 to 4) thick **asparagus spears**

1 ball of **Pizza Dough**, shaped and waiting on a floured peel (page 26)

15 grams (¼ cup) finely grated **Parmigiano-Reggiano cheese**

20 grams (about ¾ ounce) **Saint Nectaire cheese**, cut into 6 chunks

4 to 6 **quail eggs** (see Note, page 99)

Pinch of **fine sea salt**

MAKES ONE 10- TO 12-INCH PIZZA • People often find this pie to be one of my most exotic and inventive, but when I think back on the way I developed it, that's not how it seems to me at all. There was the asparagus in front of me, and I wanted to make it work for a pizza; shaving it was the answer, so it would be thin and yield to quick cooking. That looked a lot like a bird's nest to me, hence the quail eggs—and then there's the cheese, of course, pulling everything together.

(recipe continues)

1. Place the pizza stone in a gas oven on a rack about 8 inches from the broiler. Preheat the oven on bake at 500°F for 30 minutes. Switch to broil for 10 minutes. (For an electric variation, see page 18.)

2. Cut away about 2 inches of the base of each asparagus spear. With a vegetable peeler, shave the entire asparagus from bottom to top, reversing your grip and rotating as necessary to shave as much as possible. Don't rush it; be deliberate for the greatest precision. You should have about 90 grams (3 ounces) of very thin ribbons.

3. With the dough on the peel, sprinkle the Parmigiano evenly over the surface and distribute the chunks of Saint Nectaire on top. Arrange the asparagus shavings over the cheese.

4. With quick, jerking motions, slide the pie onto the stone. Broil for 2½ minutes under gas (somewhat longer with an electric oven; see page 18). The cheese should be bubbling, the crust only slightly charred.

5. Using the peel, pull the pizza out of the oven. Close the oven to conserve heat.

6. Crack the eggs very carefully to keep each yolk whole. Place the eggs around the pizza (one for each slice). Sprinkle the salt evenly over the pie. Return to the oven to broil for 1 minute, until the eggs are set but not hard and the charring is deeper.

7. Using the peel, transfer the pizza to a tray or serving platter. Slice into wedges (cutting through the egg yolks to allow them to spread slightly). Serve immediately.

NOTE If quail eggs are unavailable (farmer's markets are often an excellent source), go with the smallest eggs you can find. In the restaurant I dress up the pie more than I do here, with a slice of oil-packed truffle on each yolk. But those truffles in oil are virtually impossible to find retail. If you're feeling flush, go ahead and put a slice of truffle on each yolk or, for that matter, a drizzle of truffle oil (but not both, which would be overwhelming). In any case, the way I present it here—truffle-less—is great.

ham and cheese pie

2 grams (about 1 teaspoon) **caraway seeds**

1 ball of **Pizza Dough**, shaped and waiting on a floured work surface (page 26)

30 grams (about 1 ounce) **pecorino fresco** (see page 17), cut into ½-inch cubes and slightly flattened by pressing between thumb and index finger

18 grams (⅓ cup) finely grated **Gruyère cheese**

50 grams (about 1¾ ounces) fresh **mozzarella**, pulled into shreds

2 pinches of freshly ground **black pepper**

100 grams (7 to 10 thin slices) **prosciutto**

MAKES ONE 10- TO 12-INCH PIZZA • Ham and cheese is, of course, a commonplace combination—but this pizza will still surprise you. The caraway seeds on the bottom of the crust are there because I was, naturally, thinking of rye bread. The ham—prosciutto in this instance—is placed over all the other toppings at the end, like an uncooked blanket, and the result is miles from ordinary.

1 Place the pizza stone in a gas oven on a rack about 8 inches from the broiler. Preheat the oven on bake at 500°F for 30 minutes. Switch to broil for 10 minutes. (For an electric variation, see page 18.)

2 Sprinkle the caraway seeds over a lightly floured peel and place the shaped dough on top of it. Evenly distribute the pecorino, Gruyère, mozzarella, and pepper over the dough.

3 With quick, jerking motions, slide the pie onto the stone. Broil for 3½ minutes under gas (somewhat longer with an electric oven; see page 18), until the top is bubbling and the crust is nicely charred but not burnt.

4 Using the peel, transfer the pizza to a tray or serving platter. Drape the prosciutto evenly over the pie, completely covering the surface. Slice and serve immediately.

popeye pie

MAKES ONE 10- TO 12-INCH PIZZA • This pizza is one of my most popular dishes, a kind of warm spinach salad on a crust. I've been serving it since the earliest days at Sullivan Street (its origins—how I came to make it—are now lost in the mists of memory). But, even today, to the best of my knowledge, I'm the only one who offers it. Try it at home, and right after that first bite, you'll see why it's one of the most popular pies I've ever devised. When I make the Popeye in my home kitchen, I deviate from the usual system in this book and bake it (as called for here) rather than placing it under the broiler. The image of that mound of spinach directly under flame just seems wrong—I'm not even sure what would happen, but it wouldn't be good.

1 ball of **Pizza Dough**, shaped and waiting on a floured peel (page 26)

1 medium **garlic clove**, grated

30 grams (about 1 ounce) **pecorino fresco** (see page 17), cut into 1-inch cubes and slightly flattened by pressing between thumb and index finger

18 grams (⅓ cup) finely grated **Gruyère cheese**

50 grams (about 1¾ ounces) fresh **mozzarella**, pulled into shreds

2 pinches of freshly ground **black pepper**

120 grams (about 4¼ ounces) fresh **spinach**

Generous pinch of **fine sea salt**

Extra-virgin olive oil, for drizzling

1 Place the pizza stone in a gas oven on the middle rack. Preheat the oven on bake at 500°F for 30 minutes. Switch to broil for 10 minutes and then back to bake at 500°F. (For an electric variation, see page 18.)

2 With the dough on the peel, sprinkle the surface evenly with the garlic. Distribute the pecorino, Gruyère, and mozzarella evenly over the dough. Sprinkle evenly with pepper.

3 With quick, jerking motions, slide the pie onto the stone. Bake for 2 minutes.

4 Pull the rack partially out of the oven. Quickly add the spinach in what will look like a big mound (the spinach will reduce, the mound flattening, as spinach always does when it cooks). Sprinkle evenly with salt. Return the pie to the oven for 3½ to 4 minutes in a gas oven (somewhat longer with an electric oven; see page 18), until the crust is charred in spots, but not as deeply as with the other pizzas in this book.

5 Using the peel, transfer the pizza to a tray or serving platter. Drizzle evenly with oil. Slice and serve immediately.

NOTE The spinach I prefer—and this may come as a surprise, given how I feel about the venal corporate influence—is bagged spinach. It is cleaner than bunched spinach and labor free, a convenience product that actually makes sense. But there are still some things to keep in mind: There should be no moisture in the bag, which encourages rotting. Check for discoloration. Blackened leaves mean that the spinach in that bag has seen hard times.

shiitake with walnut puree pie

MAKES ONE 10- TO 12-INCH PIZZA • Just after multiple catastrophes decimated Japan, I, like so many others, felt I had to raise money for the recovery somehow. A fund-raiser at my restaurant and bakery turned out to be a great success. One of the chefs who showed up (along with customers, vendors, and old friends) was Jean-Georges Vongerichten, a longtime supporter of my work. I told him I'd been thinking, naturally enough, about making do in hard times, about limitations. I wanted to make a pizza that was extremely spare in its ingredients, one that contained little protein but was delicious and satisfying nevertheless. Jean-Georges is brilliant, of course, and described one he and Michel Bras, the revered French chef, had made together: this simple vegetarian pizza with a walnut-onion puree covered in sliced mushrooms.

1 ball of **Pizza Dough**, shaped and waiting on a floured peel (page 26)

100 grams (scant ½ cup) **Walnut Puree** (recipe follows)

90 grams (about 9 medium) **shiitake mushroom caps**, thinly sliced

10 fresh **rosemary leaves**

Generous pinch of freshly ground **black pepper**

4 grams (½ teaspoon) **fine sea salt**

Extra-virgin olive oil, for drizzling

1 Place the pizza stone in a gas oven on a rack about 8 inches from the broiler. Preheat the oven on bake at 500°F for 30 minutes. Switch to broil for 10 minutes. (For an electric variation, see page 18.)

2 With the dough on the peel, spoon the walnut puree over the surface and spread it evenly, leaving about an inch of the rim untouched. Distribute the mushroom slices over the puree, all the way out to the edge. Sprinkle with the rosemary, pepper, and salt.

3 With quick, jerking motions, slide the pie onto the stone. Broil for 3½ minutes under gas (somewhat longer with an electric oven; see page 18), until the crust is nicely charred. The mushrooms should be dark and thoroughly cooked but not burnt.

4 Using the peel, transfer the pizza to a tray or serving platter, drizzle it with oil, slice into wedges, and serve.

walnut puree

**MAKES ABOUT 200 GRAMS (SCANT 1 CUP),
OR ENOUGH FOR 2 PIES**

100 grams (about 1 cup)
Spanish or **white onion**,
sliced 1 centimeter (½ inch)
thick

50 grams (1⅓ cups) **walnuts**

50 grams (scant ¼ cup)
water, plus more as needed

1 Separate the onion slices into strips with your fingers
  and place them in a saucepan. Cover and cook over
  very low heat, stirring every 15 minutes or so, for
  45 minutes to 1 hour, until very soft. Uncover and set
  aside to cool.

2 Combine the onion,
  walnuts, and water in a
  blender or food processor
  and pulse until you have
  an almost smooth puree,
  something like the texture
  of oatmeal. There should
  still be a touch of the
  walnut bits remaining but
  the puree should be easily
  spreadable. If it is not, add
  a little water and continue
  blending until it is.

squash with pumpkin seeds pie

MAKES ONE 10- TO 12-INCH PIZZA • This pizza sounds like it should be served only at holidays, the way so many of us restrict turkeys and hams to special occasions. But do yourself a favor: As soon as the cool weather hits and the pumpkins and other squash start to show up, don't hold back; give it a try. Then, if you enjoy it as much as I think you will, make it a regular treat.

215 grams (7½ ounces) **kabocha squash**

10 grams (about 1 tablespoon) **extra-virgin olive oil**

10 grams (1 tablespoon) **pumpkin seeds**

1 ball of **Pizza Dough**, shaped and waiting on a floured peel (page 26)

20 grams (scant ⅓ cup) grated **pecorino fresco** (see page 17)

15 grams (¼ cup) finely grated **Parmigiano-Reggiano cheese**

Pinch of **chili flakes**

Generous pinch of **fine sea salt**

1 Place the pizza stone in a gas or electric oven on a rack about 8 inches from the broiler (no closer, even if you're using an electric broiler). Preheat the oven to 450°F.

2 Peel, seed, and quarter the squash. Slice it paper-thin and put it in a bowl. Toss with the oil to coat evenly. Spread the squash out on a half baking sheet in one layer.

3 Put the pumpkin seeds in a pie plate. Simultaneously, on the stone, bake the squash and pumpkin seeds for 10 minutes. Remove from the oven and set aside.

4 Raise the gas oven temperature (still on bake) to 500°F and continue preheating the stone for 20 minutes. Switch to broil for 10 minutes. (For an electric variation, see page 18.)

5 With the dough on the peel, distribute the pecorino and Parmigiano over the surface. Place the squash slices evenly over the cheese and season with chili flakes and salt. Broil for about 3½ minutes under gas (somewhat longer with an electric oven; see page 18), until the cheese is bubbling and the crust is well charred but not burnt.

6 With the peel, remove the pie from the oven and sprinkle with the reserved pumpkin seeds.

poached artichoke with walnut puree pie

1 ball of **Pizza Dough**, shaped and waiting on a floured peel (page 26)

100 grams (scant ½ cup) **Walnut Puree** (page 107)

75 grams (3 or 4) **Poached Artichokes** (recipe follows), cut into ½-centimeter (¼-inch) slices

10 grams (3 tablespoons) finely grated **Parmigiano-Reggiano** or **Grana Padano cheese**

Generous pinch of **fine sea salt**

MAKES ONE 10- TO 12-INCH PIZZA • The mushroom and walnut pizza (page 106) was so good, so meaty and filling—without any actual meat or even cheese—that I wanted to build on it to come up with another pie. I decided that instead of mushrooms I'd poach a few artichokes to place on top of the pie and see what happened. It worked beautifully and is really very distinct from the shiitake version.

1 Place the pizza stone in a gas oven on a rack about 8 inches from the broiler. Preheat the oven on bake at 500°F for 30 minutes. Switch to broil for 10 minutes. (For an electric variation, see page 18.)

2 With the dough on the peel, spoon the walnut puree over the surface, and spread it evenly, leaving about an inch of the rim untouched. Distribute the artichoke slices over the pie. Sprinkle with the cheese, then salt.

3 With quick, jerking motions, slide the pie onto the stone. Broil for 3½ minutes under gas (somewhat longer with an electric oven; see page 18), until the top is golden and the crust is nicely charred but not burnt.

4 Using the peel, transfer the pizza to a tray or serving platter. Slice and serve.

(recipe continues)

poached artichokes

MAKES 75 GRAMS (3 OR 4)

1 liter (1 quart) **water**

1 **lemon**, halved

200 grams (3 or 4) raw **baby artichokes**

250 grams (1¼ cups) **extra-virgin olive oil**, plus more if needed

25 grams (about 1½ tablespoons) **red wine vinegar**

Generous pinch of **fine sea salt**

1 Pour the water into a bowl. Squeeze the lemon juice into it and add the lemon halves. Add the artichokes, keeping them in the acidulated water whenever you are not working with them, so they retain their color. Remove one artichoke and pull or cut off the tough outer green leaves, leaving the stem intact. Remove any remaining discolored spots. As you do this with each artichoke, immediately put it back in the water.

2 Drain the artichokes and put them in a small saucepan. Add the oil and vinegar; the liquid should cover them completely. Bring to a simmer over medium heat. Cook for 5 minutes, then turn off the heat and let cool to room temperature. The artichokes can be drained and used immediately or refrigerated in their oil for up to 1 month. Gently warm them in a pan so the chilled oil is released before using.

NOTE When the recipe calls for baby artichokes, it doesn't simply mean the smallest ones you happen to see. The name is specific—like baby carrots. When you buy baby artichokes, the great thing about them is that the choke has only just begun to form and is completely edible, as are the leaves (once the tough ones have been removed before poaching).

pizza bianca

MAKES TWO 10- TO 12-INCH PIZZAS • I've published a version of this recipe (for a thicker pizza) elsewhere, but it's so much a part of my repertoire—and this is a pizza book, after all—that I felt it would be remiss not to include it here. Instead of baking the pie as I usually do, I decided to use the same broiling technique you see throughout this book. At Co., I offer this pizza in the menu section on breads—an indication of how much it differs from all the others—and serve it with some ricotta cheese for spreading on top. The composition of this dough differs from the one you use throughout this book in minor ways. You'll still need to begin preparing it a day ahead.

200 grams (1½ cups) **all-purpose flour**, plus more for dusting

1 gram (¼ teaspoon) **active dry yeast**

4 grams (½ teaspoon) **fine sea salt**

4 grams (¾ teaspoon) **sugar**

175 grams (¾ cup) **cool water**, plus more if needed

20 fresh **rosemary leaves**

4 grams (½ teaspoon) **coarse sea salt**

30 grams (about 3 tablespoons) **extra-virgin olive oil** for drizzling, plus more for the bowl

1 In a medium bowl, thoroughly blend the flour, yeast, fine sea salt, and sugar. Add the water and, using a wooden spoon or your hands, mix for at least 30 seconds, until you have a soft, loose dough. It should be slightly sticky; if it's not, mix in more water (up to 2 tablespoons).

2 Lightly coat the inside of a large bowl with olive oil and put the dough in it. Cover the bowl with a plate or plastic wrap and let it sit for a minimum of 9 hours and up to 12 hours at room temperature (about 72°F), until doubled in size.

3 Generously flour a work surface and scrape the dough onto it. Fold the dough over itself 2 or 3 times and split it into 2 rather flat balls. Put the dough in a warm, draft-free spot, covered with a very damp tea towel, and let rise until doubled in volume, 1 to 2 hours.

4 Half an hour before the end of the second rise, place the pizza stone in a gas oven about 8 inches from the broiler. Preheat the oven on bake at 500°F for 30 minutes. Switch to broil for 10 minutes. (For an electric variation, see page 18.)

5 Shape one of the balls into a disk, as with other pizzas (see page 29), and place it on a floured peel. Sprinkle with half of the rosemary. With the tips of your fingers, make indentations (dimples) all over the surface.

6 With quick, jerking motions, slide the dough onto the baking stone. If it's sticking to the peel, gently lift it around the edges, adding more flour to the peel. Broil until the crust is golden brown on the mounds but still pale in the dimples, about 3½ minutes.

7 Slide the peel under the pizza and transfer the pizza to a rack. Sprinkle with half the coarse salt, drizzle with half the oil, and allow to cool for at least a few minutes before slicing and serving.

8 Repeat the shaping and broiling with the second ball.

TOPPINGS

caramelized onions [118]

lardons [122]

merguez [123]

pork sausage [124]

veal meatballs [125]

red pepper sauce [127]

Here are some of the toppings and flavor building blocks I turn to again and again. I like to keep them on hand in my kitchen for when inspiration strikes. If a recipe in this book calls for Caramelized Onions, for example, or Veal Meatballs, you can certainly make them as needed, but you may well decide to prepare some of these toppings hours or even days earlier so that pizza baking can be a weeknight affair. That's what the recipes in this section allow you to do.

Also, I can't know how many pizzas (or toasts and salads) using the same ingredient you're planning to make. So these recipes almost always make a greater quantity than for just one pizza— and, frequently, offer suggestions on how else you might use whatever isn't consumed at the first meal. If you're like me, you're going to be grateful every time you realize you've got some of these ingredients waiting and ready. It's the kind of preparation that allows you to cook not just quickly but spontaneously.

caramelized onions

• It may perplex you that no sugar is added to these onions, even though I promise they will caramelize. As pungent as onions are, they actually contain a lot of sugar. The slow cooking releases the sugar as it softens and sweetens the onion slices, very gradually; the onions will take a little over an hour to prepare.

600 grams (3 medium) **onions**

3 grams (½ teaspoon) **red wine vinegar**

10 grams (about 1 tablespoon) **extra-virgin olive oil**

Leaves from 2 **thyme sprigs**

2 grams (¼ teaspoon) **fine sea salt**

1   Cut the onions in half and then into 1½-inch-thick slices. With your fingers, separate the slices into strips and put them in a medium bowl. Toss with the vinegar, oil, and thyme leaves.

2   Transfer the onions to a 10-inch sauté pan. Cover and cook, stirring every few minutes, over medium-low heat for 20 minutes. Do not burn. Uncover the pan and continue cooking, stirring occasionally, until the onions are golden and soft, about 30 minutes.

3   Sprinkle with the salt, transfer to a platter, and set aside to cool to room temperature. Use at once or cover and refrigerate for up to 5 days.

lardons

MAKES 260 GRAMS (35 TO 40 PIECES) • *Lardons* is a French term referring to thick bacon batons or dice. The fatty, smoky richness is beyond fabulous when you combine the bacon with ingredients like mozzarella. You could always buy thick-cut bacon from the supermarket, of course, but quality matters—far better to get a couple of slabs from a good butcher. When you dice the bacon, don't worry about perfect uniformity. It's fine if the chunks vary somewhat; no one is going to eat this pizza with a ruler. Besides, a little dimensional variety adds visual interest. As for uses for any leftovers, your imagination will take you all over the place, starting with salads and frittatas.

550 grams (about 1¼ pounds) thickly sliced skinless **slab bacon**

1 Preheat the oven to 400°F.

2 Slice the bacon into strips lengthwise, about ½ inch wide. Slice those strips into chunks about ½ to 1 inch long. Arrange the lardons on a baking sheet in one layer and bake for about 20 minutes (less—10 to 15 minutes—if you're using bacon slices). They should be browned but still have a bit of tender meatiness to them; in other words, you don't want crisp bacon.

3 Let the lardons cool to room temperature. If not using immediately, cover and refrigerate for up to 1 week; bring them back to room temperature before using.

merguez

40 grams (about ¼ cup) **extra-virgin olive oil**

75 grams (generous ½ cup) finely diced **Vidalia onion**

75 grams (½ cup) finely diced **celery**

2 grams (1 tablespoon) finely chopped **rosemary leaves**

2 grams (1 tablespoon loosely packed) finely chopped **fresh mint**

250 grams (9 ounces) **ground lamb**

2 grams (1 teaspoon) **sumac powder**

4 grams (2 teaspoons) **sweet paprika**

2 grams (1½ teaspoons) **chili flakes**

4 grams (about 1½ teaspoons) **fennel seeds**

3 grams (scant ½ teaspoon) **fine sea salt**

MAKES 370 GRAMS (13 OUNCES) • This lamb mixture, a staple for sausages and other preparations in North Africa, is a major element in my Pepperoni Pie (page 61), although you could just as easily form it into burgers and grill them to serve on a bun or as a breakfast side dish with eggs. It can be mixed into a pasta sauce, too. The ingredient that may be unfamiliar here is sumac powder, ground berries of the sumac bush (not the poisonous kind, you'll be glad to hear) that grows all over the Middle East. It's fruity and a bit astringent, and is available these days from many purveyors, such as Williams-Sonoma, or online. You can substitute cumin powder, but the flavor will be slightly different.

1   Heat the oil in a sauté pan over medium heat and cook the onion and celery until tender, about 5 minutes. Stir in the rosemary and mint and cook briefly until fragrant, 30 seconds to 1 minute. Transfer the mixture to a medium bowl and set aside until cool.

2   Stir in the lamb, sumac, paprika, chili flakes, fennel seeds, and salt. Use immediately or cover and refrigerate for up to 3 days.

pork sausage

MAKES 525 GRAMS (JUST OVER 1 POUND) • You're not actually going to form this mixture into sausages (although you could) but use it instead as a bright, richly flavored ground meat topping. If there's enough remaining once you've made your pizzas, brown it for a pasta sauce or form it into meatballs for a sandwich with sautéed peppers and onions on a baguette.

3 grams (1 heaping teaspoon) **fennel seeds**

500 grams (about 1 pound) ground **pork butt**

1½ **garlic cloves**, finely chopped

8 grams (1¼ teaspoons) grated fresh **ginger**

2 dried **chili peppers**, crumbled, or ½ teaspoon **chili flakes**

6 grams (¾ teaspoon) **fine sea salt**

1 Toast the fennel seeds in a dry saucepan over medium heat, shaking the pan continuously, until they just start to color and turn fragrant, 1 to 2 minutes; be careful not to burn them. Transfer to a plate to cool.

2 In a medium bowl, with your hands, mix the pork, fennel seeds, garlic, ginger, chili flakes, and salt. Set aside if you're going to prepare a pizza immediately. If not, cover and refrigerate for up to 3 days; bring back to room temperature before using.

veal meatballs

6 grams (¾ teaspoon) **fine sea salt**, plus more for the water

80 grams (½ medium) **Idaho potato**, peeled

About 500 grams (1 pound) ground **veal**

10 grinds **black pepper**

1 to 2 **garlic cloves**, finely chopped

Leaves from 3 **thyme sprigs**

25 grams (2 tablespoons) **whole milk**

13 grams (1 tablespoon) **canola oil**

MAKES 35 TO 40 MEATBALLS • When the restaurant reviewer for the *New York Times* visited Co., he singled out the meatball pizza as a favorite. Customers seem to swear by it, too. The pie (page 55), you'll see, is nothing like what you'll find at most neighborhood pizzerias. It's nuanced and something you'll always remember. And amazingly easy! If you make fewer than four or five pizzas, save the remaining meatballs for pasta or sandwiches or for serving as an appetizer (see page 56).

1 Bring salted water to a gentle boil in a medium saucepan and cook the potato until tender, 20 to 25 minutes. Drain it, then pass through a food mill into a medium bowl (or grate using a box grater). Allow to cool.

2 Add the veal, salt, pepper, garlic, thyme leaves, and milk and blend thoroughly, but gently, with your hands. With moistened hands, roll into meatballs about 1 inch in diameter. You should have 35 to 40.

3 Coat a sauté pan with the oil and brown the meatballs for 7 or 8 minutes over medium heat, until they are medium (just a bit pink in the center). Set them aside until you're ready to use them, or let cool, cover, and refrigerate for up to 4 days; bring back to room temperature before using.

red pepper sauce

15 grams (2 small) dried **pasilla peppers**, toasted under the broiler, seeded, pith removed (see Note, page 128)

350 grams (3 medium) **red bell peppers**, peeled and seeded

25 grams (1½ tablespoons) **water**

20 grams (about 1½ tablespoons) **nam pla** (fish sauce)

Combine the pasillas, bell peppers, and water in a food processor or blender and puree until smooth. Add more water if necessary. Stir in the fish sauce. Use immediately or cover and refrigerate for up to 5 days; bring back to room temperature before using.

MAKES 300 GRAMS (ABOUT ¾ CUP) • There are several fast, simple, basic, multifunctional preparations in this book, but this one may take the prize. It can be used to embellish broiled fish or chicken breast, be blended with tomato sauce for a pasta, or, as here, become the foundation for a pizza—the Pepperoni Pie (page 61). (*Pepperoni,* as I use it, doesn't refer to the sausage but its literal translation; it means "peppers" in Italian.) The unusual ingredient—for a pepper puree—is nam pla, the now familiar fish sauce. It doesn't come across as a distinct taste but is in the recipe as a flavor booster for the pepper.

NOTE Pasillas are mild, dried peppers readily available in Mexican food shops and lots of other places. Many cooks soak dried peppers; I prefer to toast them under the broiler until they steam, to soften them. Then I split them and scoop out the seeds and pith (do this quickly; as the peppers cool they tend to become dry again). If you've got a pizza stone heated in the oven, broil the peppers on that for about 20 seconds. If not, use the broiler alone and turn them once.

TOASTS, SOUPS, AND SALADS

homemade ricotta cheese 134
chicken liver toasts 135
cannellini bean toasts 137
japanese eggplant toasts 138
ripe tomato toasts 139
broccoli rabe and ricotta toasts 140
garlic scape and lovage
pesto toasts 143
gazpacho 144
pea soup 147
asparagus and avocado salad 148
escarole salad 151
radicchio salad 152

In a restaurant, you expect your customers to stay a while, sipping wine and savoring what may be several courses. Each pizza is made to order, after all, which means it will take a few minutes, even with all the toppings standing at the ready. And so we have offerings to keep the crowd occupied: toasts, soups, and salads. At home you're going to run into the same issue when friends come over, or even when you're just feeding family. I think these dishes work especially well as a preamble to the pizza ahead. For that matter, think of serving them as appetizers or at cocktail parties, even when there isn't a pizza in sight.

A NOTE ON THE TOASTS The yields all assume you'll use slices of crusty Italian bread about the size of those we offer in the restaurant, which are cut from a rustic loaf 4 or 5 inches in diameter. But this is a matter of preference. Choose slices of baguette, if you like, but you'll need more of them to use all the toast toppings. The thickness of each slice is purely a matter of preference, too. Also, you may want to halve or quarter the slices, depending on how you're serving them—as an appetizer or an hors d'oeuvre.

homemade ricotta cheese

MAKES 220 GRAMS (7½ OUNCES) • Ricotta cheese, like a lot of great foods (bread comes to my baker's mind immediately, of course) is the product of what is often described as "controlled spoilage." In this case, you acidify fresh milk and cook it so that it curdles, breaking into creamy curds (the cheese) and a thin whey. The cheese is beautifully versatile—for desserts, pastas, or all by itself. At the restaurant, I like to serve it alongside Pizza Bianca (page 112) to be spread on top or eaten as a side dish. Ricotta, by the way, means "cooked twice," and you'll see why as you do just that.

1 liter (1 quart) **whole milk**

80 grams (⅓ cup) cultured **buttermilk**

Pinch of **fine sea salt**

1 In a saucepan over medium heat, gently stirring, bring the whole milk to 160°F. Remove from the heat and allow to cool to 120°F. Stir in the buttermilk. Cover the pan and allow the mixture to stand at room temperature for 6 to 12 hours. The milk will acidify but should not start to curdle.

2 Add the salt and gently reheat the mixture until it reaches a simmer. Curds will form (if they don't, the acidification time was inadequate—allow the mixture to cool and reheat it).

3 Place cheesecloth—folded once—in a colander or strainer. Pour the mixture through it to drain away the whey and leave only the cheese behind. Allow the cheese to cool to room temperature. Cover and refrigerate for up to 3 days.

chicken liver toasts

10 grams (about 1 tablespoon) **extra-virgin olive oil**

120 grams (1 cup) diced **onion**

60 grams (½ cup) chopped **shallots**

60 grams (scant ½ cup) chopped **celery**

1 **bay leaf**

Fine sea salt

Coarsely ground **black pepper**

45 grams (⅓ cup) diced **apple**

15 grams (about ¼) unpeeled medium **lemon**, cut into 2 slices, seeded, and diced

15 grams (1½ tablespoons) drained **capers**

10 grams (about 1½ fillets) **salt-packed anchovies** (see page 17), rinsed and dried

115 grams (4 ounces) **chicken livers**, rinsed, patted dry, and excess fat and veins removed

90 grams (scant ⅓ cup) **sweet wine**, such as Riesling or Marsala

6 to 8 slices crusty, slightly stale **Italian bread**, toasted

1 **garlic clove**, peeled

MAKES 6 TO 8 TOASTS •

In the Italian town of San Casciano dei Bagni, I have a lot of old friends whom I met for the first time when I was a very young baker. We all got together thanks to the graciousness of the restaurateur Joe Allen (once a benefactor of mine and kind of royalty there), who invited me to use his house nearby. Silvestro Boni, part of the most prominent family in town, taught me to make a liver spread using the organs of veal, pig, and chicken. Back in the States, I figured I was better off just sticking with chicken liver as part of a spread that uses a few sweet ingredients to mute the power of the liver. I even like to mix shallots with onion— that might seem redundant, but shallots are sweeter and milder.

1 In a large heavy saucepan, heat the oil over low heat until hot. Add the onion, shallots, celery, and bay leaf, along with a sprinkle of salt and pepper. Cook, stirring occasionally, until wilted, about 20 minutes. Be careful not to let the vegetables burn.

2 Add the apple, lemon, and capers. Continue to cook, shaking the pan and stirring occasionally, for about 3 minutes. Add the anchovies and livers. Do not stir; you want the livers to brown and the anchovies to break down. Cook for about 2 minutes.

3 Add the wine, stirring to dissolve the brown bits adhering to the bottom of the pan. Cook for 3 to 4 minutes to burn off the alcohol. Remove the bay leaf.

4 Scrape the mixture into a blender or food processor and pulse until the mixture is almost a puree but still has just a bit of texture. (If it seems too thick and pasty, add water to achieve the desired smoothness.) Scrape the liver mixture into a container. Taste and season with salt and pepper, if necessary.

5 Rub one side of each toast with the garlic and spread with a generous amount of the liver mixture.

cannellini bean toasts

250 grams (1¼ cups) dried **cannellini beans**

300 grams (about 1½ cups) plus 7 grams (about 2 teaspoons) **extra-virgin olive oil**

120 grams (1 cup) diced **onion** (¼-inch dice)

60 grams (½ cup) diced **celery** (¼-inch dice)

60 grams (½ cup) diced **carrot** (¼-inch dice)

20 grams (about 3 fillets) **salt-packed anchovies** (see page 17), rinsed and dried

1 small **bay leaf**

Pinch of **chili flakes**

60 grams (about 2½ ounces) **slab bacon**, cut into ¼-inch dice

200 grams (⅞ cup) **water**

6 to 8 slices crusty, slightly stale **Italian bread**, toasted

1 **garlic clove**, peeled

Fine sea salt

MAKES 6 TO 8 TOASTS •

Diners and cooks of some accomplishment have tasted this dish and marveled at it. "What does he do?" one food writer asked. But, friends, there's no mystery; this dish is simply beans blended with one of the most classic of combinations: chopped onions, celery, and carrot, a French standby called a *mirepoix*. And then come a few ingredients more commonly associated with Italian cooking: anchovies, chili flakes, and olive oil. This can be a little messy to eat—a bean or two always insists on rolling off the toast—but when you taste it, I don't think that will bother you at all.

1 Put the beans in a large bowl and add enough cold water to cover by at least 2 inches. Let soak overnight.

2 In a medium heavy saucepan, heat the 7 grams (2 teaspoons) oil over low heat until hot. Add the onion, celery, and carrot. Cook, stirring, until tender, about 6 minutes. Add the anchovies, bay leaf, and chili flakes and continue to cook, stirring occasionally, for another 2 minutes.

3 Stir in the remaining oil, the bacon, and water. Drain the beans and add them to the saucepan. Bring the mixture to a boil and then lower the heat. Simmer, covered, until the beans are tender but not mushy, about 2½ hours. Remove the bay leaf.

4 Rub each piece of toast on one side with the garlic clove. Place a heaping spoonful of the bean mixture on each toast and sprinkle with salt to taste.

japanese eggplant toasts

MAKES 6 TO 8 TOASTS

• The Japanese eggplant, slender and purple, is sweet to begin with because it has fewer seeds than many of its larger brethren, and seeds provide a lot of an eggplant's bitterness. Here, its sweetness is further enhanced and brightened by a touch of ginger and lemon juice. Charring the eggplant before peeling it adds an element of smokiness.

600 grams (about 4) **Japanese eggplants**

2 grams (¼ teaspoon) grated fresh **ginger**

2 grams (scant 1 teaspoon) freshly squeezed **lemon juice**

4 grams (½ teaspoon) **fine sea salt**, plus more for sprinkling

6 to 8 slices crusty, slightly stale **Italian bread**, toasted

1 **garlic clove**, peeled

Extra-virgin olive oil, for drizzling

14 **cilantro leaves**, thinly sliced

1 Put the eggplants on a baking sheet as close to the broiler as possible and broil, turning once, until charred, 8 to 10 minutes. Set aside to cool, then peel away the skin with your fingers. Coarsely chop the eggplant and transfer it to a medium bowl.

2 Stir in the ginger, lemon juice, and salt. Taste the eggplant and adjust the seasoning, if necessary.

3 Rub each toast on one side with the garlic and top with a heaping tablespoon of the eggplant mixture; drizzle with oil. Sprinkle with a pinch of salt and a touch of cilantro.

NOTE You might wonder why I use "slightly stale" bread for the toast. First, it's an excellent way to use bread that might otherwise be wasted; second, a little bit of staleness seems to enhance the texture, making it pleasantly chewy. But there's nothing to stop you from simply toasting fresh bread.

ripe tomato toasts

475 grams (just over 1 pound) ripe **tomatoes**

Ground chili to taste

6 to 8 slices crusty, slightly stale **Italian bread**, toasted

1 **garlic clove**, peeled

5 medium **basil leaves**, roughly torn

Extra-virgin olive oil, for drizzling

Fine sea salt

1. Cut away the stem areas of the tomatoes, core them, and coarsely dice them, cutting gently to preserve their juices. Place in a bowl.

2. Sprinkle the tomatoes with ground chili (how much you'll need will depend on how flavorful the tomatoes are).

3. Rub each toast on one side with the garlic and top with tomato and basil. Drizzle with olive oil and sprinkle with salt. (Again, if the tomatoes are not absolutely great, they will need more salt; if perfect, don't overwhelm the flavor.) Don't let the toasts stand for more than a few minutes before serving, or they'll begin to get soggy.

MAKES 6 TO 8 TOASTS

• This is definitely an in-season sort of thing. I know I've sung the song of the tomato elsewhere in this book, and here also ripe, flavorful tomatoes are emphatically key. But if they're not absolutely perfect—even unavoidably subpar—you can remedy the problem somewhat by seasoning them more assertively. Basically, as you'll see, this toast represents only a slight variation on the ubiquitous combination of tomato with basil. Whoever introduced these two world travelers to each other (the tomato, originally from South America, and the basil, originally from Asia) deserves a commemorative statue. I add a touch of chili and garlic. That's enough to bring the fabulous partnership one step further.

broccoli rabe and ricotta toasts

MAKES 6 TO 8 TOASTS •
This toast is an appealing exercise in counterpoints. The broccoli rabe is slightly bitter and has a texture that fights back as you bite through it. The dried pepper is sharp. All that makes the ricotta seem softer, even creamier, than it normally would be.

150 grams (about 6 stalks) **broccoli rabe**

Fine sea salt

17 grams (scant 1½ tablespoons) **extra-virgin olive oil**, plus more for drizzling

2 large **garlic cloves**, sliced ⅛ inch thick plus 1 **garlic clove**, peeled

Chili flakes

6 to 8 slices crusty, slightly stale **Italian bread**, toasted

40 grams (3 tablespoons) **ricotta** (page 134)

Coarsely ground **black pepper**

2 grams (½ teaspoon) grated **lemon zest**

1 Trim and discard any discolored or wilted leaves and trim tough stems from the broccoli rabe and rinse it.

2 Bring a medium saucepan of salted water to a boil. Meanwhile, fill a medium bowl with ice and cold water and have it waiting on a work surface. Blanch the broccoli rabe in the boiling water for about 20 seconds, until bright green. Transfer it immediately to the ice bath to halt the cooking. Drain, pat it dry, and set aside.

3 Heat 10 grams (1 tablespoon) of the oil in a saucepan, add the sliced garlic and a pinch of chili flakes, and cook for 30 seconds. Tear the broccoli rabe into 2-inch pieces and add to the pan. Cook, shaking the pan continuously, for about a minute. Transfer the mixture to a platter and allow to cool.

4 Rub each toast on one side with the garlic clove. Spread the ricotta over the toast and season generously with black pepper. Arrange the broccoli rabe over the toast. Sprinkle with the lemon zest, chili flakes, and salt and drizzle with the remaining oil.

garlic scape and lovage pesto toasts

125 grams (½ cup) chopped **garlic scapes**, or a mixture of 20 grams (2 tablespoons) chopped **garlic** plus 50 grams (½ cup) coarsely chopped **scallions**

15 grams (¼ cup) finely grated **Parmigiano-Reggiano cheese**

45 grams (about ⅓ cup) toasted **pine nuts**

105 grams (½ cup) **extra-virgin olive oil**

10 grams (about ⅓ cup) chopped **lovage**, or 15 grams (2½ tablespoons) chopped **celery**

2 grams (about ¼ teaspoon) **fine sea salt**

12 grams (about 1 tablespoon) freshly squeezed **lemon juice**

6 to 8 slices crusty, slightly stale **Italian bread**, toasted

1 **garlic clove**, peeled and halved

MAKES 6 TO 8 TOASTS •

This toast is mysterious to many people. The two main ingredients are not that widely known, even though they're fast becoming farmer's market stalwarts. A scape is the thin shoot you see growing out of garlic (not the thick leaves of green garlic) and it's milder than the garlic itself. Lovage is a vegetable that tastes a lot like celery, but it's heartier and has more character. As you'll see in the recipe, I think garlic, celery, and scallions work well as substitutes here if either scapes or lovage—or both—aren't available. The result is just a little less special. In any event, you'll create a toast that is brilliant green and stunning on the table. Note that you'll probably have more pesto than you need for the toasts, but it's really good stuff, so use the rest on pasta or anything else that works for you.

1   Combine the scapes, Parmigiano, pine nuts, and 65 grams (about ¼ cup) of the oil in a food processor. Pulse until smooth. Add the lovage and salt. Pulse to blend. Add the remaining olive oil and keep blending until the mixture is almost pureed but still has a chunky texture. Stir in the lemon juice. Taste the mixture and adjust for seasoning, if necessary.

2   Rub each toast on one side with the garlic and top with a thin spread of the scape mixture. (Think of it as a smear rather than a heavy topping.) Cut the toasts into bite-sized servings.

gazpacho

SERVES 4 • I've made gazpacho many times and many different ways. This version is the one we're currently serving at the restaurant. It's spicier and smokier than most other recipes, thanks to the poblano peppers and the bonito flakes I've been enamored of lately.

80 grams (½ large) **green bell pepper**

85 grams (1 medium) **poblano chili pepper**

1 kilo (about 2 pounds or 5 large) ripe **tomatoes**, cored and quartered

300 grams (1 medium) **cucumber**, peeled, seeded, and chopped

2 medium **garlic cloves**, peeled

36 grams (⅔ cup) **plain bread crumbs**

15 grams (1 tablespoon) **red wine vinegar**, or more to taste

10 grams (about 1½ teaspoons) **fine sea salt**, or more to taste

Dried, aged **bonito flakes** for sprinkling

Fresh **basil leaves**, green or purple, for serving

1 Char the bell and poblano peppers over the flame of a gas range or under the broiler, turning several times, until blackened all over. Peel, seed, and coarsely chop the peppers; set aside.

2 Put the tomatoes in a food processor and blend until roughly pureed. Set a fine-mesh strainer over a bowl and force the tomato puree through it. Discard the remaining solids and seeds.

3 Return the tomato puree to the food processor. Add the peppers, cucumber, garlic, bread crumbs, vinegar, and salt and puree until smooth. Adjust the seasoning with additional salt and vinegar if necessary.

4 Serve the gazpacho chilled, topped with the bonito flakes and basil leaves.

NOTE Bonito flakes are available in Asian specialty stores or online.

pea soup

25 grams (about 2 table-spoons) **extra-virgin olive oil**, plus more for drizzling

80 grams (generous ½ cup) diced **white** or **yellow onion**

2 large **garlic cloves**, thinly sliced

14 grams (1 tablespoon) **fine sea salt**, or to taste

700 grams (3 cups) **water**

5 grams (about 20) whole fresh **mint leaves**

450 grams (1 pound) frozen **peas**, defrosted

1 thick slice rustic, stale **bread**, toasted and cut into croutons

Grated **Parmigiano-Reggiano cheese**

SERVES 4 • The story behind this soup is as straightforward as you can imagine. It was April in New York and my corporate chef, Matt, was thinking about green things. This pea soup may sound too elemental, but when gussied up with mint it's great; I put it on the menu almost as soon as the first spoonful was out of my mouth. The recipe uses frozen peas—a good idea when you need a significant quantity. The flavor is all there, but the labor isn't.

1 Combine the oil, onion, garlic, and salt in a medium pot and cook over low heat until the onion is tender, about 2 minutes; it should not take on any color.

2 Add the water and bring to a boil. Add 3 grams (a little more than half) of the mint and continue boiling for 1 minute. Remove from the heat and set aside to cool. Chill the soup base until cold.

3 Transfer the soup base to a blender, add the peas, and puree until smooth. The soup is best served slightly chilled.

4 Garnish the soup with the croutons, a drizzle of oil, and a sprinkling of Parmigiano. Chop the remaining mint and sprinkle it over the soup.

asparagus and avocado salad

SERVES 4 • The beauty of this salad is that it is vibrant proof that some terrific ingredients simply deserve each other, even if the partnership doesn't come to mind immediately. A cookbook-writing friend came to the restaurant one day, ordered this asparagus and avocado combo, tasted it, and kept muttering, "Genius, genius!" Not me. Nature did it.

160 grams (4 or 5) thick **asparagus spears**

1 **avocado**, halved, pitted, and peeled

16 fresh **mint leaves**, chopped

½ **lime**

20 grams (about 2 tablespoons) **extra-virgin olive oil**

Pinch of **fine sea salt** per serving

1 Cut away about 2 inches of the base of each asparagus spear. With a vegetable peeler, shave the entire asparagus from bottom to top, reversing your grip and rotating as necessary to shave as much as possible. Don't rush it; be deliberate for the greatest precision.

2 Divide the asparagus strips among 4 salad plates. Cut each avocado half into 4 sections and place 2 wedges on each salad. Sprinkle with the mint leaves. Squeeze lime juice over the salads, drizzle evenly with the oil, and sprinkle with salt.

escarole salad

127 grams (1 cup) finely chopped **shallots**

50 grams (9 to 12 fillets) **salt-packed anchovies** (see page 17), rinsed and dried

Juice of 1 **lemon**

Generous pinch of **fine sea salt**

75 grams (about ⅓ cup) **extra-virgin olive oil**

320 grams (1 head, about 11 ounces) **escarole**, stems removed, washed and dried

Dried plain **bread crumbs**, for sprinkling

21 grams (about 2 tablespoons) drained **capers**

SERVES 4 TO 6 • It's my version of a Caesar salad—I switch escarole for romaine and omit the egg. If you're a fan of the classic, I'm sure you'll love this, too.

1 In a food processor, combine the shallots, anchovies, lemon juice, salt, and oil. Blend, pulsing, until pureed.

2 Chop the escarole coarsely, place in a medium bowl, and combine with some of the dressing. The leaves should be coated with dressing, not swimming in it.

3 Arrange the salad on individual plates and sprinkle with the bread crumbs and capers.

radicchio salad

SERVES 4 • The star here is really the Taleggio, a soft, mild (despite the pungent aroma), fruity cheese that Italians frequently pair with radicchio, as I do here. The cheese is often grated, but I like the way the chunks look on the plate and how they allow the flavor of the cheese to stand out.

280 grams (1 medium head) **radicchio**, sliced into ½-inch strips

20 grams (3 tablespoons) **balsamic vinegar**

30 grams (about 3 tablespoons) **extra-virgin olive oil**

2 grams (¼ teaspoon) **fine sea salt**

113 grams (4 ounces) **Taleggio cheese**

80 grams (about 8 medium) **shiitake mushroom caps**, thinly sliced

Divide the radicchio among individual plates. Drizzle with the vinegar and oil and sprinkle with the salt. Break the cheese into ¾-inch chunks and arrange them around each plate. Top with the sliced mushrooms.

sucrine lettuce salad

SERVES 4 • Like so many others today, I'm often a market-driven cook: I like to see what's available at the farmers' stalls and work around that. Sucrine is a little-known lettuce that's been turning up more frequently and quickly becoming a favorite of New York City chefs. It's a summertime jewel in the eastern United States and a fall item in the West. Sucrine is actually a variety of romaine that in some ways also resembles bibb. The name is derived from the French word for sugar, and it does have a gentle sweetness about it. The other components of the salad are also mostly sweet and mild. In this case I turn to a very spicy vinaigrette as the counterpoint.

> **NOTE** If sucrine is not available, substitute baby romaine.

About 140 grams (1 ear) shucked **corn on the cob**

320 grams (about 11 ounces) **sucrine**, washed and halved

115 grams (about 4 ounces) **blackberries** (or raspberries), halved

120 grams (about 12) **cherry tomatoes**, halved

½ **avocado**, pitted, peeled, and cut into 1-inch chunks

50 grams (about ¼ cup) **Spicy Vinaigrette** (recipe follows)

2 grams (¼ teaspoon) **fine sea salt**

1 Remove the corn kernels with a paring knife in strips about 2 inches long and 2 kernels wide.

2 Bring a small pot of salted water to a boil. Add the corn and boil for 3 minutes. Drain and set aside to cool.

3 Divide the lettuce halves among individual plates. Strew the blackberries, tomatoes, and avocado artfully over each portion of lettuce. Add the corn to the salads. Drizzle each salad with the vinaigrette and sprinkle with salt.

spicy vinaigrette
MAKES 490 GRAMS (2 CUPS)

200 grams (about 1 cup) **extra-virgin olive oil**

100 grams (about 1 medium) stemmed and seeded **red bell pepper**, roughly chopped

70 grams (¼ cup) **red wine vinegar**

50 grams (scant ¼ cup) **lime juice**

40 grams (2 tablespoons) **sriracha** (Thai hot sauce)

16 grams (2 teaspoons) **nam pla** (fish sauce)

5 grams (generous ½ teaspoon) **fine sea salt**

Combine the oil, bell pepper, vinegar, lime juice, sriracha, nam pla, and salt in food processor or blender and blend until smooth.

baby octopus salad

1 to 2 large **oranges**, as needed

8 whole **baby octopuses**, cleaned and thoroughly dried

20 grams (a scant 2 tablespoons) **extra-virgin olive oil**

Fine sea salt

36 grams (about 1¼ ounces) **purslane**, left in clusters of two or three

14 grams (1 stalk) **celery heart**, sliced ⅛ inch thick on the bias

4 medium fresh **mint leaves**, roughly torn

4 medium fresh **basil leaves**, roughly torn

45 grams (about ¼ cup) **Pink Peppercorn Dressing** (recipe follows)

SERVES 4 • This is a traditional Italian offering, with a few twists of my own. I use purslane, for instance, which is a weed but also a wonderful green, related to cactus. It grows well in arid climates because of its ability to store water. It's very similar in taste to arugula but more sour and less peppery (some people find it slimy and, if you're one of them, you may simply prefer arugula in its place). Purslane is much more widely sold these days than it used to be—either at farmer's markets or organic food stores. I choose pink peppercorns, rather than black, for the dressing because they're less harsh and a better complement for the citrus in the salad. The orange sections leap out in both color and taste.

1 Slice off the top and bottom of one of the oranges. Stand it upright and slice away the peel and pith until the flesh is exposed. Cut between the membranes to release the segments. You want 16. Repeat with a second orange if needed.

2 Heat a grill or cast-iron pan over high heat until hot. Coat the octopus with the oil and sprinkle with salt. Grill, turning occasionally, until charred and tender, around 4 minutes.

3 While the octopus is cooking, arrange the purslane, celery, mint, basil, and orange segments on individual plates or on a platter. Season with salt.

4 Cut each octopus in half and distribute the pieces on top of the salad. Drizzle the dressing over the top.

(recipe continues)

NOTE "Baby" octopus really means baby. You want the smallest you can find. The ones we use are about 2 inches in diameter. A good source is Asian markets. Our tester, Amanda, found hers in a local Thai market.

pink peppercorn dressing

MAKES 90 GRAMS (½ CUP)

6 grams (2 or 3 strips) **orange zest**, removed with a peeler

50 grams (scant 3 tablespoons) freshly squeezed **orange juice**

40 grams (about 2½ tablespoons) freshly squeezed **lemon juice**

8 grams (1½ teaspoons) **champagne vinegar**

5 grams (about 1 teaspoon) **extra-virgin olive oil**

8 grams (1 tablespoon) **pink peppercorns**

2 grams (1 teaspoon) finely diced **jalapeño pepper**

2 grams (¼ teaspoon) **fine sea salt**

1 Put the zest in a small saucepan and cover with cold water. Bring the water to a boil, then drain. Repeat the process two more times. Dry thoroughly.

2 In a small food processor or blender, blend the zest, orange juice, lemon juice, vinegar, oil, peppercorns, jalapeño, and salt until smooth.

melon salad

SERVES 4 • It's a culinary axiom that we eat with our eyes as well as our mouths. That's especially true with this dish. It takes what may strike you as overfamiliar components (prosciutto and melon) and then enhances their beauty (and flavor) with the deep purple of blackberries and the green of basil. The arrangement matters here. Make each plate as beautiful as you can. And when you serve it, be sure everyone knows to try to get as many of the individual elements as possible in each mouthful—a bit of melon, a little of the berry, a touch of basil. That's how the combination comes alive.

1 small ripe **cantaloupe** or other melon

40 grams (¼ cup) **extra-virgin olive oil**

Fine sea salt

4 grams (1½ teaspoons) freshly squeezed **lime juice**

8 large fresh **basil leaves**

12 **blackberries**, halved

150 grams (about 12 thin slices) **prosciutto**

Freshly ground **black pepper**

1 Peel, halve, and seed the melon. Slice it thinly, and arrange about 5 slices, overlapping, to cover each of 4 appetizer plates. Drizzle 1 tablespoon of the oil over each serving. Sprinkle with salt and drizzle with the lime juice. Tear 2 basil leaves over each portion.

2 Arrange the blackberry halves on each plate, spaced gracefully. Roughly tear the prosciutto slices and place the pieces in half-moons (or, to take another image, single parentheses) between the berries. Finish with a sprinkling of pepper. Serve chilled.

shiitake, celery, and parmesan salad

200 grams (about 20 medium) **shiitake mushroom caps**, thinly sliced

200 grams (4 medium stalks) **celery**, strings removed and cut into batons 3 inches long and ¼ inch thick

Juice of ½ **lemon**

15 grams (1½ tablespoons) **extra-virgin olive oil**

Generous pinch of **fine sea salt**

Freshly ground **black pepper**

15 grams (scant ¼ cup) shaved **Parmigiano-Reggiano cheese**

SERVES 4 • Salads like this are among my simplest. Sliced shiitakes and celery together make a fresh, delicate pair that do not need to be messed with any further.

In a bowl, toss together the mushrooms, celery, and lemon juice. Divide the salad equally among 4 plates. Drizzle with the oil and sprinkle with salt and pepper. Top with the shaved Parmigiano and serve.

kale and brown rice vinegar salad

90 grams (about 3 ounces) peeled **celery root**

32 grams (about 3 tablespoons) **extra-virgin olive oil**, plus more for drizzling

Pinch of **fine sea salt**, plus 4 grams (½ teaspoon)

90 grams (about 3 ounces) peeled and cored **apple**

210 grams (about 7½ ounces) dark green **kale**, stemmed and torn into 2-inch pieces

45 grams (4 tablespoons) **brown rice vinegar**

SERVES 4 • Ordinarily you wouldn't think of turning to raw kale for a salad; the leaves are just too tough. But the vinegar in this recipe does the job that cooking would, breaking down the leaves. And I've chosen brown rice vinegar rather than its plainer rice relative because the brown variety is richer and more flavorful.

1 Preheat the oven to 500°F.

2 Cut the celery root into batons about 2 inches long and ½ inch thick. Drizzle them with oil and sprinkle with a pinch of salt. Place them on a baking sheet in a single layer and bake for 6 to 8 minutes, until golden and creamy soft but not mushy.

3 Meanwhile, roughly cut the apple or slice into batons, the same shape as the celery root.

4 In a large bowl, toss together the celery root, apple, kale, 32 grams (about 3 tablespoons) oil, vinegar, and 4 grams (½ teaspoon) salt and allow to rest for 8 to 10 minutes. The kale should be al dente—that is, offer some resistance but still be tender enough to bite through without tearing at it.

roasted squash and pumpkin seed salad

SERVES 4 • Roasted squash is a deeply flavorful addition to a salad, but it's the toasted crushed pumpkin seeds that make this dish. I like to just break the seeds into roughly shaped pieces between my fingers. They add a distinctive flavor and crunch that elevate this salad, basic as it is, way beyond what many others can offer.

160 grams (5½ ounces) **butternut** or **kabocha squash**, peeled and cut into 1½-inch pieces (1 cup)

125 grams (about ⅔ cup) **extra-virgin olive oil**

32 grams (¼ cup) **pumpkin seeds**

50 grams (¼ cup) fresh **lemon juice**

Coarse salt

280 grams (1 head, about 10 ounces) **bibb lettuce**, quartered

Freshly ground **black pepper**

1 Preheat the oven to 450°F.

2 Toss the squash with a teaspoon or so of the olive oil on a baking sheet. Roast until tender and lightly colored, 15 to 20 minutes. Set aside.

3 In a sauté pan over medium-low heat, toast the pumpkin seeds, stirring or flipping, until puffed and browned. (You could also place them in a separate pan in the oven while the squash is roasting.) Set aside.

4 In a small bowl, whisk together the remaining oil, the lemon juice, and a generous pinch of salt until thoroughly emulsified.

5 Arrange the squash and lettuce on each plate. Sprinkle with salt and pepper. Crush the pumpkin seeds over the top.

6 Spoon a tablespoon or two of the lemon dressing over each serving.

salt-crusted beet salad with lemon dressing

400 grams (1½ cups) **kosher salt**

2 large **egg whites**

25 grams (1½ tablespoons) **water**

8 grams (about 1½ teaspoons) **red wine vinegar**

Leaves from 1 **thyme sprig**

360 grams (4 small) **beets**, tops and tails removed

125 grams (about ⅔ cup) **extra-virgin olive oil**

50 grams (about ¼ cup) fresh **lemon juice**

8 grams (1 teaspoon) **fine sea salt**, or to taste

80 grams (about 3 ounces) **watercress**, tough stems removed

15 grams (½ cup packed) fresh **mint leaves**

Crushed **pumpkin seeds**, for serving (optional)

SERVES 4 • Beets, cooked until tender and placed on a bed of lettuce, are a nice enough salad with no other embellishment. This recipe is only a little more involved, but the reward is great: Baking beets in a salt crust intensifies their flavor, trapping the juices. The watercress and mint give the salad a sophisticated touch.

1 Preheat the oven to 450°F.

2 In a bowl, stir together the kosher salt, egg whites, water, vinegar, and thyme leaves until the mixture resembles wet sand.

3 Cover each beet completely in the salt crust mixture and put on a baking sheet. Bake until tender, about 1 hour. Let the beets cool, then remove the crust, peel, and cut into 2-inch chunks.

4 In a small bowl, whisk together the oil, lemon juice, and fine sea salt until fully emulsified.

5 Arrange the beets on individual plates and dress with the lemon vinaigrette. Top with the watercress and mint. Sprinkle with pumpkin seeds, if desired.

mozzarella and tomato salad

SERVES 4 • This salad is my version of the caprese (named after Capri), certainly one of the most popular Italian salads of all. I haven't done much to it, except show it some respect and give it my own sense of composition. Often when you see this salad, the tomatoes and cheese are in thick slices; I prefer to cut them into chunks and then arrange on the plate as artfully as I can.

230 grams (8 ounces) fresh **mozzarella**, cut into chunks

230 grams (8 ounces) ripe **tomato**, cut into chunks

40 grams (¼ cup) **extra-virgin olive oil**

4 grams (½ teaspoon) **coarse sea salt**

Freshly ground **black pepper**

10 fresh **basil leaves**

Lightly toss the mozzarella and tomato together. Arrange on 4 plates, drizzle with oil, and sprinkle with salt and pepper. Tear the basil leaves over the top and serve.

poached artichoke salad

60 grams (about 2 ounces) **arugula**

Double batch of **Poached Artichokes** (page 111)

40 grams (¼ cup) **extra-virgin olive oil**

15 grams (about 1 tablespoon) fresh **lemon juice**

Pinch of **fine sea salt**

Freshly ground **black pepper**

40 grams (about ¼ cup) drained brined **capers**, chopped

20 grams (about ¼ cup) shaved **Parmigiano-Reggiano cheese**

SERVES 4 • I serve this salad regularly at the restaurant, and I think part of what makes it so popular is that it's so beautiful. The poached artichokes, the same ones that are on my Shiitake with Walnut Puree Pie (page 106), are a touch exotic. But even better, when I composed this salad in my mind, I knew the flavors would work wonderfully even before I tasted it. And they do.

Divide the arugula among 4 plates. Distribute the artichoke quarters on top. Blend the oil and lemon juice and drizzle over the salad. Sprinkle with the salt, pepper, capers, and cheese shavings. Serve.

pea shoot salad

SERVES 4 • Some people say pea shoots taste like grass. I think they taste like spring and maybe you will, too. Regardless, just add some sliced red radish to them and you have another brilliantly beautiful thing to set out on the table that requires, oh, two or three minutes to prepare. You'll notice I'm very sparing with the lemon juice, which is meant to brighten the salad but not acidify it.

120 grams (4½ ounces) **pea shoots**

120 grams (4 medium) **red radishes**, thinly sliced

12 grams (generous 1 tablespoon) **extra-virgin olive oil**

Juice of ½ **lemon**

Fine sea salt for sprinkling

In a bowl, toss the pea shoots, radishes, and olive oil together very lightly. Divide the salad among 4 plates and dress each one with some drops of lemon juice and a sprinkling of salt.

anchovy dip for crudités

160 grams (about 5½ ounces) **salt-packed anchovies** (see page 17), rinsed and dried

1 medium **garlic clove**, chopped

260 grams (about 1¼ cups) **extra-virgin olive oil**

175 grams (¾ cup) **water**

30 grams (about 2½ tablespoons) freshly squeezed **lemon juice**

2 grams (¼ teaspoon) **fine sea salt**

Crudités of your choice

1 Combine the anchovies, garlic, oil, water, lemon juice, and salt in a blender and, scraping down the sides with a spatula, blend until very smooth.

2 Serve in a small bowl set in the middle of a platter, surrounded by crudités.

MAKES 700 GRAMS (ABOUT 3 CUPS) • If you're one of those people with an aversion to anchovies, this dip may help you get over it; it's a remarkable concoction—smooth, with bite and character. There is no overpowering anchovy taste. It's meant as a dip for crudités such as carrots, kohlrabi, radishes, and celery. I know crudités often seem more ornamental than anything else, because many people just don't eat them. This dip will ensure otherwise. Any leftover dip will be terrific as a dressing for a green salad.

NOTE When I specify using a blender (and don't mention a food processor, as here) it's because a blender is by far the best choice for creating a dip that's creamier and lighter than it would be made any other way.

Banoffee Pie

DESSERTS

vanilla gelato 176
summer berry sundae 178
milk chocolate sundae 179
my chocolate chip cookies 180
olive–olive oil cake 182
banoffee pie 183

The pizzas you've met in this book more often than not have some bite to them, whether it's the heat of chili, the spice of sausage, or simply the acid of tomato. It's no wonder that diners crave some dessert at the end—a sweet, smooth leavening of the palate. Simple egg-enriched gelato might do the job, but it's not heavy; it's light and cold and comforting. Really good cooking always resonates with the familiar, even when it's been so reinvented that the familiar part is hidden somewhere. And we've become conditioned to expect a dessert to announce the end of a meal. It feels right. Here are a few suggestions, mostly drawn from the desserts that are served at the restaurant.

vanilla gelato

MAKES 1 LITER (ABOUT 1 QUART) • This main gelato recipe is the basic vanilla version we use at the restaurant. The creative urge will drive you to vary and build on it—as we did in the five variations that follow. After all, the same approach (without the vanilla) can be turned to countless familiar but terrific and simple desserts. Just let your imagination do the walking and create your own flavors. There are also a couple of sundaes here—gussied up versions of the unadorned gelatos—one a super-rich chocolate version and the other light and bright as a summer day, bursting with berries. They bring a dollop of showmanship to the gelato repertoire.

1 liter (1 quart) **whole milk**

1 **vanilla bean**, split lengthwise and scraped, or 6 grams (1 teaspoon) vanilla extract

3 large **egg yolks**

150 grams (about ⅔ cup) **sugar**

1 Combine the milk and vanilla bean and seeds (if using extract, add it later) in a saucepan and bring to a simmer.

2 Prepare an ice bath, setting a large bowl inside an even larger bowl half full of ice water.

3 In a bowl, whisk the egg yolks and sugar until bright yellow. Temper them by blending in about one-quarter of the heated milk. Pour the mixture into the saucepan and, over low heat, whisking continuously to prevent sticking and overcooking the eggs, bring to 180°F (or until the mixture coats the back of a spoon and remains separated when you draw your finger through it).

4 Strain through a fine-mesh sieve into the chilled bowl and cool in the ice bath until cold. If using vanilla extract, add it now.

5 Follow the directions on your home ice cream maker to freeze the gelato.

chocolate gelato

Omit the vanilla. Melt 110 grams (4 ounces) semisweet chocolate and 28 grams (1 ounce) unsweetened chocolate. Stir into the still-warm gelato mixture before chilling and then freezing in your ice cream maker.

peach gelato

Omit the vanilla. Add 220 grams (1 cup) finely chopped peeled peach (to remove the skin, drop the peach in boiling water for 10 to 15 seconds and then peel it with a paring knife) to the gelato base after it is chilled and before freezing in your ice cream maker.

coffee gelato

Omit the vanilla. Dissolve 24 grams (¼ cup) instant espresso in 114 grams (¼ cup) warm water. Stir into the still-warm gelato mixture before chilling and then freezing in your ice cream maker.

milk chocolate gelato

Omit the vanilla. Melt 175 grams (6 ounces) milk chocolate and stir into the still-warm gelato mixture before chilling and then freezing in your ice cream maker.

corn gelato

Omit the vanilla. Remove milk from the heat. Steep 2 corn cobs (remove the kernels first and save them for another use) in the hot milk for 15 minutes. Strain, then mix in the egg mixture and proceed with the recipe.

summer berry sundae

SERVES 8 • The two elements of this sundae that may well separate it from every other one you've had are the corn flavoring of the gelato and the Marcona almonds, which make for a fascinating partnership. Your palate is going to be aware of just the slightest bit of corn, but the Spanish almonds—they strike me as more buttery than the common roasted almonds—latch on to that corn flavor and enhance it just as actual butter goes so well with corn on the cob. This is most definitely a summer sundae.

220 grams (1 cup) **heavy cream**

16 grams (1 tablespoon) **sugar**

Corn Gelato (page 177)

140 grams (1 cup) **mixed summer berries** (whatever is available)

140 grams (1 cup) crushed **Marcona almonds**

1 Whip the cream with the sugar until it forms soft peaks.

2 To serve, place 3 scoops of gelato in each of 8 bowls. Top with whipped cream, berries, and a sprinkling of crushed almonds.

milk chocolate sundae

60 grams (⅓ cup) **sugar**

275 grams (1¼ cups) **heavy cream**

Chocolate Gelato (page 177)

76 grams (½ cup) **salted peanuts**

40 grams (¼ cup) **pomegranate seeds**

1   Prepare the caramel sauce: Put the sugar in a heavy saucepan and bring to a boil over medium heat. Cook, swirling the pan once the sugar begins to color, until quite dark but not smoking. Carefully stir in 55 grams (¼ cup) of the cream; the hot caramel will splatter. Remove from the heat.

2   Whip the remaining 220 grams (1 cup) cream until it holds soft peaks.

3   To serve, place 3 scoops of gelato in each of 8 bowls. Top with whipped cream, peanuts, and pomegranate seeds. Drizzle caramel sauce over the top.

SERVES 8 • Gelato topped with whipped cream and caramel sauce is going to be terrific no matter what, but very familiar. With this sundae I add a couple of frills that, in my view, turn it into more of an event. The salted peanuts bring crunch and a savory counterpoint to balance the pronounced sweetness of the sundae. But the pomegranate seeds take it even further. They're juicy, with a hint of tartness. And despite how rapidly they're gaining in popularity these days (countless fans proclaim their supposed health virtues), they're still just exotic enough to get people around the table talking about this sundae instead of simply inhaling it.

my chocolate chip cookies

MAKES 30 COOKIES •
If you've baked chocolate chip cookies before, the first thing you'll probably notice about this recipe is how relatively hot the oven is. Two things are accomplished at 500°F: The cookies cook much faster and they achieve a bit of crispness on the outside while remaining soft and delicate on the inside. I also use quite a lot of chocolate chips. Seems to me if you're going to call these chocolate chip cookies, that's what should dominate them.

150 grams (10 tablespoons) **unsalted butter**, softened

75 grams (⅓ cup packed) **brown sugar**

75 grams (scant ⅓ cup) **granulated sugar**

1 large **egg**, at room temperature

150 grams (1 cup plus 2 tablespoons) **all-purpose flour**

2 grams (½ teaspoon) **baking powder**

2 grams (¼ teaspoon) **coarse sea salt**

180 grams (1 cup) **semisweet chocolate chips**

1 Preheat the oven to 500°F.

2 In an electric stand mixer on high speed, beat together the butter and sugars for 2 to 3 minutes. The mixture should look like thick whipped cream. Add the egg and beat for 30 seconds.

3 In a separate bowl, mix together the flour, baking powder, and salt. Working by hand with a spatula, completely incorporate the flour mixture and chocolate chips into the butter-sugar mixture.

4 Line a baking sheet with parchment paper and distribute heaping teaspoons, about 20 grams each, at least 1½ inches apart (the cookies will flatten and spread as they cook). Bake for 6 to 7 minutes, watching them carefully. They should be crisp on the edges and soft on the inside.

olive–olive oil cake

MAKES ONE 9-INCH CAKE

• Olive oil cake is a tradition in parts of Italy, often citrus-infused (as here), a cousin to a sponge cake and famous for staying moist for days. When I was coming up with one, I wanted to sprinkle something a little extra into the batter and my eye ran around my restaurant's kitchen. Blueberries seemed like a decent idea. But then I spotted the olives—not briny ones, but the oil-cured kind, which would still be fruity and not salty. The idea seemed like it could be over the top. But maybe not . . . it turned out even better than I'd hoped.

Unsalted butter for the pan

Flour for the pan

5 large **eggs**

245 grams (1 cup plus 2½ tablespoons) **granulated sugar**

290 grams (generous 1⅓ cups) **extra-virgin olive oil**

260 grams (2⅔ cups) sifted **cake flour**

7 grams (1¾ teaspoons) **baking powder**

4 grams (½ teaspoon) **fine sea salt**

Grated zest of 1 medium **orange**

60 grams (about 22) pitted black, **oil-cured olives**, sliced

Confectioners' sugar, for dusting

1 Preheat the oven to 325°F. Butter the sides and bottom of a 9-inch cake pan and flour the bottom, tapping out excess.

2 Using an electric stand mixer, beat the eggs and granulated sugar until smooth. Add the olive oil and fully incorporate it. On low speed, blend in the cake flour, baking powder, salt, and orange zest. Remove the bowl from the mixer and fold in the olives.

3 Using a spatula, scrape the batter into the pan and bake for 45 minutes. Pierce the center of the cake with a toothpick to check it; the toothpick should come out clean when done. If it doesn't, bake for up to 15 minutes more, checking every 7 minutes or so.

4 Let the cake cool in the pan for about 30 minutes, then invert it onto a rack to cool completely. Turn it back over. Dust the top with confectioners' sugar and serve.

banoffee pie

113 grams (1 stick) **unsalted butter**, melted

225 grams (1 cup) **graham cracker crumbs** (pulverized in a food processor)

10 grams (2 teaspoons) **granulated sugar**

500 grams (about 2 cups) **heavy cream**

25 grams (¼ cup) **confectioners' sugar**

2 drops **coffee extract** or 2 generous pinches **instant espresso**

3 ripe **bananas**, peeled and sliced into rounds

60 grams (generous ⅓ cup) **hazelnuts**, crushed and toasted

MAKES ONE 9-INCH PIE

• This pie is a traditional English dessert. But never mind. We serve it at our intensely Italian restaurant because this coffee and banana treat, rich and sweet, turns out to be a beautiful punctuation to a meal centered around pizza.

1 Preheat the oven to 400°F.

2 To prepare the crust, combine thoroughly in a bowl the butter, graham cracker crumbs, and granulated sugar. Press the mixture evenly over the bottom and sides of a 9-inch pie plate. Bake for 8 minutes. Set aside to cool.

3 Combine the cream, confectioners' sugar, and coffee extract in a mixing bowl and whip until medium peaks form.

4 Cover the crust with sliced bananas and top with the whipped cream. Sprinkle with the hazelnuts. Best served and eaten that day, but can be refrigerated for 1 day.

ACKNOWLEDGMENTS

I HAVE TO THANK first and foremost Rick Flaste, whose thoughtfulness and skill made putting this book together so much fun. The guy's a real sage.

This book owes so much to the staff at my New York restaurant, Co., that I want to express my deepest gratitude for the assistance (in the book as well as the restaurant) of my corporate chef, Matt Aita, a truly brilliant and gifted cook. Matt was often joined in everything we did by my chef de cuisine, Brendan Corr.

My personal assistant during the period when this book was being written was Liz Elzi. Without her diligence and eagerness, the work would have gone a whole lot less smoothly.

Away from the restaurant, in her home kitchen, toiling rapidly, efficiently, and with great intelligence, was Amanda McDougall. She tested every recipe in the book, corrected errors when she found them, and when the recipes weren't as clear as they might be suggested how to fix them. Others who pitched in were Jeff Bieda, Emily McKenna, and Ian Knauer.

Although Squire Fox is already credited here as the photographer, he and his crew worked so closely and intensely with me and Rick that I will always be grateful to him for the beauty he brought to my work. Maya Joseph, always at my side, gave the manuscript a careful, caring reading, and for that I offer my fondest thanks.

Rica Allannic, our skilled editor, managed to remain cheerful and gracious throughout this project even when the going got a trifle rough. Equally fine to work with was her assistant editor, Ashley Phillips. Thanks, also, to Stephanie Huntwork, Robert Siek, and Kim Tyner at Clarkson Potter.

Our agent and steadying hand, Janis Donnaud, stood behind us throughout the project as well as the one that preceded it, *My Bread*. Her support was invaluable.

And, of course, none of this would have been possible without the backing and unwavering encouragement of my business partners, the chef Jean-Georges Vongerichten and the restaurateur Phil Suarez.

My mother Cecelia's love and faith in me has nourished me throughout this book and my career.

INDEX